FOOTPRINTS IN THE SILENT TEARS

Complex Interplay Between Love and Emotion

G.S.G

Chennai • Bangalore

CLEVER FOX PUBLISHING
Chennai, India

Published by CLEVER FOX PUBLISHING 2024
Copyright © G.S.G 2024

All Rights Reserved.
ISBN: 978-93-67076-76-7

This book has been published with all reasonable efforts taken to make the material error-free after the consent of the author. No part of this book shall be used, reproduced in any manner whatsoever without written permission from the author, except in the case of brief quotations embodied in critical articles and reviews.

The Author of this book is solely responsible and liable for its content including but not limited to the views, representations, descriptions, statements, information, opinions and references ["Content"]. The Content of this book shall not constitute or be construed or deemed to reflect the opinion or expression of the Publisher or Editor. Neither the Publisher nor Editor endorse or approve the Content of this book or guarantee the reliability, accuracy or completeness of the Content published herein and do not make any representations or warranties of any kind, express or implied, including but not limited to the implied warranties of merchantability, fitness for a particular purpose. The Publisher and Editor shall not be liable whatsoever for any errors, omissions, whether such errors or omissions result from negligence, accident, or any other cause or claims for loss or damages of any kind, including without limitation, indirect or consequential loss or damage arising out of use, inability to use, or about the reliability, accuracy or sufficiency of the information contained in this book.

Thanks to Everyone

Sponsored By

"Footprints in the Silent Tears" encapsulates centuries of human history, navigating the complex interplay between love and emotion.

Contents

Prologue vi

1. Silicon Valley of Tamilnadu 1
2. Echoes of the Classroom 4
3. Whispers On the Mind 9
4. Deadline Drama 13
5. Reflections of Motherhood 16
6. Finding Solace 20
7. Farewell Day Revelations 24
8. Journey of Hope 30
9. Echoes of Compassion 37
10. Whispers in the Night 40
11. Rainy Day Resilience 46
12. Facing the Future 49
13. Newly-Weds on the Road 52
14. Bearing Life 55
15. Women's Rebirth 58
16. From Smiles to Cries 63
17. Disparity in Recognition 70

Contents

18. The Weight of Emotions 74
19. From Tension to Tranquillity 79
20. Tessy's Pride, Aravind's Success 84
21. Through Thick and Thin 88
22. Unseen Struggles 90
23. Psychologist (Not Psychiatrist) 94
24. A Beacon Of Hope 98
25. Beyond the Edge 101
26. Alone in the Dark 105
27. The Divorce Battle 108
28. The Motorcycle Ride 111
29. A Mountain Homecoming 116
30. Love Across Generations 122
31. Rediscovering Roots 126
32. Misty Mountains and Jungle Encounters 130
33. Close Calls and Courage 133
34. Back To Reality 139
35. The Realities 142
36. The Happy Space 145
37. Seeking Resolution 149
38. Rising Star Cricket Club 151
39. The Trophy of Triumph 154
40. The Courtroom Confrontation 158
41. Tessy's Tough Choice 162

42. Navigating Custody Battles 166
43. Reflections on Uncertainty 170
44. Bonding Moments 175
45. The Burden of Pretense 178
46. The Unexpected Outcome 181
47. One Last Request 185
48. God's Verdict 191

Acknowledgements 195
Author Bio 196

Prologue

*I*n the vast expanse of time, countless creatures have inhabited the Earth, each living according to their nature. Lions hunt, dogs roam, and fish swim, all following the patterns set by their ancestors. But unlike these creatures, humans have constantly evolved beyond their natural capabilities. From the discovery of fire to the invention of the wheel, the rise and fall of kingdoms, and the advancements in technology, humans have forged a path of progress.

Yet, with each step forward, humans find themselves grappling with their own emotions and desires. Love and conflict have shaped their journey, pushing them to both greatness and despair. In today's technological world, humans stand at the precipice of losing touch with their capacity for love and empathy.

Amidst the rush of progress, there is a call for humanity to reconnect with what truly matters. We must remember that despite our advancements, our essence lies in our ability to love and empathize with one another. Only by understanding this can we heal the fractures in our society and ensure a brighter future for all.

Human life is like shooting arrows in the dark, where the main problem lies in our inability to understand others' pain while

Prologue

expecting others to understand ours. In the hustle and bustle of life, humans are running instead of walking, disrupting the emotions they carry. A healthy society requires true love and valuing others' emotions, which seems to be missing nowadays. Four characters, Tessy, Aravind, Sanjay, and Amal, will provoke different questions in your heart.

This real story, which has evoked various emotions in me over the past ten years, is one I wish to convey to people who journey through life with love and emotion.

Part 1

SILICON VALLEY OF TAMILNADU

13TH JUNE 2019

In the heart of Chennai's bustling IT hub, the OMR (Old Mahabalipuram Road) emerges as a vibrant artery pulsating with life. It's a symphony of motion, a kaleidoscope of colours, and a collision of contrasts that defines the city's complex tapestry.

As the clock strikes 8 o'clock in the morning, the OMR awakens from its brief slumber, ready to embrace another day of relentless activity. Stretching for 28 kilometers from the prestigious IIT Madras to the suburban expanse of Kelambakkam, this thoroughfare is a lifeline for the city's tech-savvy denizens.

On the surface, the roadway teems with a ceaseless procession of vehicles—gleaming sedans, sleek motorcycles, and rickety auto-rickshaws jostle for space amidst the cacophony of honking horns. Pedestrians dart across the road, navigating the chaotic flow with practiced ease, while towering skyscrapers loom overhead, their glass facades reflecting the morning sun.

Parallel to the roadway, the metro train glides effortlessly along its elevated tracks, offering commuters a respite from the gridlocked streets below. Inside the air-conditioned compartments, passengers are cocooned in a world of their own, their faces illuminated by the soft glow of smartphones and tablets.

Amidst this bustling landscape, the scent of luxury mingles with the aroma of street food, creating an olfactory symphony that is uniquely Chennai. Expensive perfumes waft from the windows of luxury cars, intermingling with the spicy aroma of freshly brewed filter coffee from roadside stalls.

Yet, for all its prosperity, the OMR is not immune to the stark realities of life. At every traffic signal, beggars and small salesmen converge, their outstretched hands a poignant reminder of the city's persistent inequalities. Here, amidst the gleaming skyscrapers and bustling thoroughfares, poverty finds a place alongside prosperity, weaving its own thread into the intricate fabric of urban life.

In this vibrant tableau, the OMR emerges as more than just a road—it's a microcosm of Chennai itself, a place where the past and present collide, and where dreams are forged amidst the relentless rhythm of city life.

As the vibrant yellow school bus, adorned with the name "St. Xavier CBSE School," makes its way along the bustling OMR, a sense of youthful energy permeates the air. Inside, rows of boys and girls, clad in their crisp school uniforms, chatter animatedly, their faces alight with the innocence of childhood.

Unaware of the complexities of the world outside, the children are enveloped in a cocoon of blissful ignorance, their minds filled with dreams and aspirations. Through the bus windows, they catch glimpses of the city's vibrant streetscape—gleaming skyscrapers, bustling marketplaces, and the ceaseless flow of traffic.

As the bus veers off the OMR onto the East Coast Road, a hush falls over the young passengers, replaced by a palpable sense of excitement. Here, amidst the urban sprawl, lies another facet of Chennai's beauty—the breathtaking proximity to the sea.

The bus traverses the winding road, flanked by swaying palm trees and panoramic views of the azure sea. Beneath them, the waters of the river bridge glisten in the morning sun, a testament to the timeless ebb and flow of nature.

Entranced by the spectacle before them, the children press their faces against the windows, their eyes wide with wonder. For them, the journey to school is not just a mundane routine—it's an adventure, filled with moments of awe and discovery.

Finally, the bus arrives at its destination—the verdant campus of St. Xavier CBSE School, nestled amidst a lush canopy of trees. As the children spill out onto the school grounds, their laughter echoes through the air, a testament to the joy of youth and the boundless possibilities that lie ahead.

As the school day began, a procession of buses made their way into the St. Xavier CBSE School grounds. Among them was the familiar yellow bus, carrying a group of excited children.

Part 2

ECHOES OF THE CLASSROOM

At the entrance stood a serene statue of heavenly mother Mary, her outstretched arms welcoming all who entered. Beside her, the head sister, dressed in a simple brown gown, offered a silent prayer, her hands clasped in reverence.

The sight of the statue and the head sister's prayer set a peaceful tone for the day ahead. Children filed off the buses, their chatter subdued by the solemnity of the moment.

The school grounds buzzed with activity as students greeted each other and made their way to their morning assemblies. Yet, amidst the hustle and bustle, there was a sense of tranquillity—a reminder of the sacredness of learning and the importance of starting the day with a moment of reverence. They followed the head sister's lead, bowing their heads in quiet reflection before dispersing to their classrooms.

As the morning sun filtered through the classroom windows, Miss Sowmiya, the science teacher, entered the room. With her bubbly demeanour and glasses perched on her nose, she exuded an air of both warmth and authority. Today, she had a twinkle in her eye as she prepared to teach the Grade 1 class.

Miss Sowmiya's lesson for the day was on different types of birds and their unique calls. With animated gestures, she explained the characteristics of each bird, mimicking their chirps and tweets to the delight of her young audience.

Amal, a mischievous boy with a shock of black hair, small eyes, and a playful grin, sat at the back of the class. His restless energy often got him into trouble, but his curiosity and creativity knew no bounds. His eyes wandered to the window, where he could see the trees swaying gently in the breeze. He listened intently to the birds outside, their melodic songs drifting into the classroom.

Miss Sowmiya noticed Amal's distraction and gently called out to him, "Amal, what are you doing over there?" Startled, Amal quickly stood up, his cheeks flushing with embarrassment. He mumbled an apology, his eyes downcast as he returned his attention to the lesson.

"What are you doing, Sowmiya asked?" Amal remained silent, unsure of what to say. Despite being caught, he didn't seem afraid.

Sowmiya persisted, asking Amal if he knew what she was teaching. Again, Amal remained silent. Sowmiya explained that she was teaching the sounds of different birds and how to recognize them. Suddenly, in a childlike voice, Amal piped up, saying he was just looking outside, catching everyone off guard.

Sowmiya, realizing that the children were amused by Amal's response, became frustrated. She raised her voice and punished

Amal by making him stand on the bench. Amal looked around at his friends, silently obeying Sowmiya's command.

As Sowmiya resumed teaching, a crow outside started cawing loudly. Amal couldn't resist looking outside again. Sowmiya noticed and became even more tense. She instructed Amal to go and call his brother.

Amal slowly left the classroom, leaving Sowmiya to continue the class.

As Amal made his way to the Grade 4 class, his steps were slow and deliberate, hoping to somehow make time speed up. When he finally reached the classroom door (Grade IV), he hesitated before entering.

Inside, Mr. Vinod, the math teacher, stood at the blackboard, his tall and collegiate appearance belying the seriousness with which he taught algebra. His words were a blur of formulas and equations, delivered with a stern focus that commanded attention.

At the front row of the class, Sanjay sat with impeccable posture, his shirt and trousers perfectly pressed, his hair neatly combed and slicked back. His height, typical for a 9-year-old boy, denoted his growing frame, with a sturdy sports body. Sanjay's appearance was neat and tidy, though not particularly striking or attractive. He diligently copied down notes, his handwriting precise and meticulous, reflecting his obedient and studious nature.

Outside the classroom, Amal called out to his brother, hoping to catch Sanjay's attention without disrupting the lesson. Sanjay, ever vigilant, noticed Amal's gestures and silently motioned for him to come in and ask permission from his teacher. But before

Amal could ask permission, Mr. Vinod's keen gaze fell upon Amal.

"What do you want?" Mr. Vinod asked his tone firm but not unkind.

Amal, his nerves frayed by the unexpected attention, replied with utmost politeness. "My teacher called my brother Sanjay, sir," he explained.

Understanding the situation, Mr. Vinod nodded and gestured for Sanjay to accompany Amal. With a quick exchange of glances, Sanjay gathered his belongings and followed his brother out of the classroom, leaving Mr. Vinod to resume his lesson on algebraic equations.

As Sanjay hurried to Amal's classroom, he found Miss Sowmiya already there, her expression stern as she addressed him.

"Sanjay, your brother Amal has been repeatedly disrupting the class," she explained, her voice firm but not unkind. "He's not listening, being disobedient, and causing a disturbance for the other children. Please inform your mother about this behaviour."

Sanjay's face darkened with a mix of frustration and concern as he listened to Miss Sowmiya's words. He knew his brother could be mischievous at times, but he hadn't realized the extent of Amal's disruptions.

"Okay, ma'am," Sanjay replied, his tone serious as he made a mental note to speak with his mother about the situation. With a nod of acknowledgment, he turned on his heels and quickly made his way back to his classroom.

Though his mind was racing with thoughts of how to address the issue with his brother and his mother, Sanjay couldn't shake the feeling of responsibility weighing heavily on his shoulders. As he entered his classroom, he resolved to find a way to help Amal understand the importance of listening and behaving in class, knowing that family support and guidance would be crucial in shaping his brother's behaviour for the better.

Part 3

WHISPERS ON THE MIND

As the school bell chimed at 4:00 PM, signaling the end of another day of classes, a flurry of activity erupted among the students. They dashed out of their classrooms, eager to secure their favourite seats on the buses waiting outside.

Among them were Amal and Sanjay, who made a beeline for Bus Number 3, their designated ride home to Kelambakkam. This bus, with its familiar route and friendly atmosphere, had become a beloved part of their daily routine.

Amal quickly found his seat in the fifth row, next to his friend Aakash. With a mischievous grin, Aakash handed Amal a neatly folded paper boat, a tradition they had developed for their bus rides home.

As the bus made its way along the route, it eventually reached the bridge where traffic often came to a standstill. Seizing the opportunity, Amal leaned out of the window, his heart pounding with excitement, and gently released the paper boat into the flowing river below.

To his delight, the paper boat glided gracefully across the water, mimicking the movements of a real boat. Amal watched with wonder as it bobbed and weaved through the currents, a tiny vessel navigating its way through the bustling cityscape.

Meanwhile, Sanjay, sitting a few rows back, observed the scene and Sanjay became increasingly concerned as he watched his younger brother Amal engage in unnecessary activities from the last row.

As the traffic signal turned green and the bus picked up speed once more, Amal settled back into his seat, a satisfied smile playing on his lips. For him, these fleeting moments of joy were a reminder that even amidst the hustle and bustle of city life, there was always room for a little bit of magic.

As the bus made its way along the route, children began to reach their respective destinations, one by one. Amal watched as his friend Aakash disembarked at Sholinganallur, waving goodbye before disappearing into the crowd.

With each stop, the bus grew emptier until only a few passengers remained, including Amal and Sanjay. Amal glanced over at his brother, who sat quietly in the last seat, gazing out the window with a distant look in his eyes.

Sensing an opportunity, Amal approached his brother's seat, his heart pounding with nervousness. "Sanjay," he whispered, trying to get his brother's attention. But Sanjay remained silent, lost in his thoughts.

Undeterred, Amal persisted, his voice growing more urgent. "Sanjay, please listen," he pleaded, his words tinged with desperation. "Don't tell Mom about what happened at school today, okay? Please."

But Sanjay remained impassive, his silence a barrier between them. As the bus rumbled on, it finally reached their stop—the Springs Lake View Apartments in Kelambakkam.

With a heavy heart, Amal stepped off the bus, his mind swirling with unanswered questions. He glanced back at his brother one last time, but Sanjay's expression remained unreadable, his secrets locked away behind a wall of silence. And as they made their way home together, Amal couldn't shake the feeling that their bond had been irrevocably changed by the events of the day.

As Amal and Sanjay entered Springs Lake View Apartments, they were greeted by the sight of the towering 13-floor building, its orange and white facade standing out against the backdrop of the nearby lake. The hustle and bustle of residents coming and going filled the air, adding to the lively atmosphere of the complex.

In the entrance area, a small room served as the watchman's station. There, they found Peter, the stern-faced watchman with a towering height, a bushy Mustache, and a bald head. Despite his imposing appearance, Peter greeted the children with a warm smile and asked how their day had been.

"Going good," Amal replied, offering a polite nod before he and Sanjay continued on their way. They passed by the bustling basketball court, where younger girls played vigorously, while elderly residents strolled leisurely through the nearby park area.

Further along, they encountered young people chatting animatedly in the cafeteria, adding to the lively ambiance of the complex. Finally, they reached the elevator, where Sanjay moved to press the button for the 6th floor, but before he could do so, Amal stepped in and insisted, "I'll do it for you, brother." With a smile, he pressed the button, and the elevator began its ascent, stopping at each floor along the way.

When they reached the 6th floor, Amal and Sanjay stepped out and made their way to their apartment, number 616. Sanjay retrieved a key from his bag, unlocked the door, and together they entered their home for the evening, ready to unwind and relax after a long day.

Part 4

DEADLINE DRAMA

*A*s the clock struck 5:30 PM, the bustling IT office of Coretronix Techno Solutions on the 9th floor of the IT Park in Sholinganallur SIPCOT was abuzz with activity. The expansive building, boasting 20 floors, housed a myriad of IT companies, ranging from local startups to global giants from Silicon Valley, USA.

Inside the office, a diverse workforce of people from various age groups, states, and religious backgrounds diligently worked at their computers. Among them was Tessy, a 32-year-old woman of Malayali origin, has a youthful appearance with sparkling eyes and chubby cheeks. Her forehead and nose are features of beauty at their peak. Tessy's ponytail hair, neatly tied back, denotes her straightforward nature. She typically wears jeans with a kurta and high heels chappals, reflecting her modern yet traditional style. At her desk, adorned with a statue of Jesus, her deep religious faith is reflected, adding to her character's depth and complexity.

As a team leader at Coretronix Techno Solutions, Tessy managed a team responsible for software development projects for an American-based chain of hotels called EUCA International

Group of Hotels. Despite the demanding nature of her job, Tessy exuded an air of calm and professionalism, guiding her team with wisdom and expertise.

Throughout the office, the hum of conversation in various languages filled the air, creating a vibrant and dynamic atmosphere. From the click-clack of keyboards to the occasional ring of a phone, the sounds of productivity echoed through the corridors of the IT Park, a testament to the hard work and dedication of its inhabitants.

Tessy received a call from her manager, Mr. Gagan Gupta, known for his short stature and arrogant demeanour. He ordered a small correction for tomorrow's client presentation, causing Tessy to feel a surge of tension.

With only half an hour left before she had to leave, Tessy knew she didn't have time to call her team members for assistance. Making the correction herself was the only option if she wanted to catch her cab, scheduled to depart promptly at 6:10 PM.

Working feverishly on her computer, Tessy's face remained serious as she kept a watchful eye on the time. With every passing minute, the pressure mounted. Yet, she remained focused, determined to finish the task before her deadline.

As the clock struck 6:00 PM, Tessy completed the correction and reported back to her manager. Hurriedly collecting her belongings, she made her way to the elevator, knowing she had little time to spare.

At precisely 6:10 PM, Tessy stepped out of the lift and rushed to the cab area. Just as she feared she might miss her ride, her teammate Karthick intercepted the cab and signalled for the driver to wait.

Breathless with relief, Tessy climbed into the cab, settling into the window seat as it pulled away from the curb. As the cab merged onto the OMR, Tessy allowed herself to relax, feeling grateful for her teammate's timely intervention and looking forward to a peaceful journey home.

As the bus pulled into Springs Lakeview Apartments in Kelambakkam, Tessy gathered her belongings and made her way towards the exit door. In the middle of the bus, she noticed her teammate Karthick, his hair adorned with a headband, sitting with one leg up on the seat as he listened to music from a Tamil movie.

The song playing was "June Ponal July Katre" from the movie "Unnale Unnale." Tessy paused for a moment, touched by the gesture of her colleague helping to get bus on time.

Turning back to Karthick, Tessy offered a heartfelt "thanks" for his assistance earlier. Karthick, with a smile, simply nodded and replied, "It's okay."

With a sense of gratitude and camaraderie, Tessy finally reached her stop and stepped off the bus, feeling grateful for the small acts of kindness that had made her journey home a little brighter.

Part 5

REFLECTIONS OF MOTHERHOOD

As Tessy entered Springs Lakeview Apartment, she greeted the watchman warmly, exchanging pleasantries before making her way to the elevator. The watchman noted her arrival and informed her that her children had already returned home. Tessy smiled and thanked him before heading upstairs.

Once inside her apartment, Tessy decided to treat her children to some snacks from the cafeteria. She purchased vegetable puffs with extra sauce, a slice of cake, and a packed coffee for herself. With the goodies in hand, she made her way to apartment number 616.

Upon ringing the doorbell, Tessy was greeted by her son Sanjay, who eagerly opened the door. The siblings shared a warm embrace, happy to see each other after a long day apart. Tessy then handed over the snacks to her children, who eagerly accepted them with gratitude.

As they settled onto the sofa together, Tessy explained that she hadn't had time to prepare any snacks at home that day, so they would have to make do with the store-bought treats. Without hesitation, the children eagerly tore into the wrappers, savouring the delicious Flavors of the snacks as they enjoyed a cozy evening together with their mother.

As Amal indulged in his puff with extra sauce, he couldn't help but notice the tension emanating from his brother, Sanjay. Sensing his brother's anger, Amal paused mid-bite, his eyes flickering with apprehension. In silent gestures, he implored Sanjay not to divulge his mischievous antics to their mother.

However, Tessy, noticing the unease between her sons, raised her voice slightly, urging Sanjay to eat quickly. Taking his cue from his mother's tone, Sanjay reluctantly began to eat, albeit with a lingering air of resentment.

Meanwhile, Amal resumed eating, his initial enjoyment overshadowed by the fear of his secrets being exposed. Tessy, sensing the tension, took a moment to sip her hot coffee before retreating to the balcony.

In the serene ambiance of the balcony, Tessy found solace amidst her small collection of plants. The sight of the lake, with its bustling avian life, brought a sense of tranquillity as she watched the bird's flit among the trees.

Lost in her thoughts, Tessy savoured the warmth of her coffee, allowing herself to relax in the soothing embrace of nature. However, her peace was short-lived as Sanjay broke the silence, eagerly recounting Amal's misadventures in school and on the bus.

Tessy's heart sank as she listened to Sanjay's revelations, her worry for Amal growing with each passing word. Despite her efforts to create a peaceful environment, the spectre of Amal's misbehaviour loomed large, casting a shadow over their otherwise serene evening.

As Tessy moved from the balcony, her disappointment simmered beneath the surface, overshadowing the tranquillity of the evening. As Sanjay began to explain Amal's misdeeds at school, Tessy's irritation grew, her frustration stemming from a deeper well of concern for her son's behaviour.

Unable to contain her emotions any longer, Tessy's anger boiled over, her voice sharp as she addressed Amal. "Amal, go and kneel down until I say so," she commanded, her tone firm with authority. Turning to Sanjay, she instructed him to focus on his studies, hoping to redirect the energy of the tense atmosphere.

Sanjay, obediently, turned his attention to his books, while Amal reluctantly complied with his mother's order, his expression a mix of defiance and resentment towards his brother for revealing his secrets.

As Tessy retreated to the kitchen, the clatter of pots and pans providing a stark contrast to the strained silence that hung in the air. Though her heart ached with disappointment, she knew that discipline was necessary to address Amal's behaviour and instil a sense of accountability.

In the kitchen, Tessy's mind raced with conflicting emotions, torn between her love for her sons and her frustration at Amal's repeated misbehaviour. As she busied herself with preparing food, she hoped that the discipline she imposed would help Amal understand the gravity of his actions and encourage him to make better choices in the future.

As Tessy finished cooking roti with egg curry, she couldn't help but feel a pang of sadness as she observed her sons. While Sanjay diligently focused on his homework at the dining table, Amal remained asleep in a kneeling position, albeit in an awkward and uncomfortable manner.

Feeling a rush of maternal instinct, Tessy called Sanjay to the dining table to eat. As Sanjay helped himself to chapati and egg curry, Tessy served herself and settled on the floor next to Amal. With gentle hands, she lifted Amal into her lap, cradling him tenderly as he slept.

Despite his slumber, Tessy softly encouraged Amal to eat, but he murmured a sleepy apology. Undeterred, Tessy carefully fed Amal, guiding the food into his mouth as he continued to sleep soundly.

With her children fed and content, Tessy finally allowed herself to eat, savouring each bite of her meal in the quiet companionship of her sleeping sons. After finishing her food and completing her chores, Tessy joined her children in bed, wrapping them in a warm embrace as they drifted off to sleep.

In the peaceful embrace of her family, Tessy found solace and comfort, knowing that despite the challenges they faced, their love for each other would always prevail. And as she drifted off to sleep, Tessy felt grateful for the simple moments of togetherness that made their bond even stronger.

Part 6

FINDING SOLACE

As Sunday morning dawned, Amal eagerly dressed in colourful shirts and trousers, his excitement palpable. However, Sanjay showed little interest in getting ready, remaining seated in a chair despite Tessy's urging. Frustrated, Tessy scolded Sanjay, emphasizing the importance of punctuality for their plans.

With determination, Tessy called for an auto, which arrived promptly in its yellow hue. Instructing the auto driver to take them to St. Luke's Orthodox Syrian Church, located near the Vellore Institute of Technology campus in Chennai, Tessy settled into the backseat.

During the journey, Tessy couldn't help but smile as she watched college students enjoying their Sunday, their laughter and camaraderie filling the air with a sense of joy and vitality.

Upon reaching the church, Tessy admired the red cross atop the church's roof, a symbol of faith and hope. The church itself, constructed from square rocks, exuded a timeless beauty as people streamed inside, eager to begin their Sunday worship.

As Tessy and her sons entered the church, she felt a sense of peace wash over her, grateful for the opportunity to spend this sacred day with her family in prayer and reflection.

As Tessy entered the church, she was greeted by the sight of wooden benches, a testament to the church's age and history. The doors, adorned with welcoming wooden frames and painted white, exuded a sense of warmth and tradition. Portraits of Jesus and Mary adorned the walls, each one telling a story of faith and devotion.

Taking her seat near the back of the church, Tessy and Sanjay listened attentively as the father spoke about the importance of love and care in the eyes of God. They offered their prayers in a disciplined manner; their hearts open to the words being spoken.

However, Amal's attention seemed to wander, his eyes drawn to the world outside the church walls. Despite the vintage charm of the wooden benches, Amal remained restless, his gaze fixated on something beyond the stained-glass windows.

As the prayers concluded, a girl moved through the congregation, collecting offerings for God. Tessy placed a hundred rupee note into the red-covered pot, a symbol of her gratitude and devotion.

With the service over, Tessy made her way outside, accompanied by her sons. As they stepped into the sunlight, Amal's eyes lit up with excitement as he spotted someone in the distance. Without hesitation, he dashed forward, his heart filled with joy as he embraced the person he had been waiting to see.

As Amal spotted a figure in the distance, his heart raced with excitement. The man, Aravind, stood tall and strong, his presence glowing with an aura of warmth and familiarity. Amal dashed forward, his arms outstretched, as he embraced the man he called daddy.

Aravind's face lit up with a radiant smile as he welcomed Amal's embrace. Each week, Aravind showered Amal and Sanjay with chocolates, toys, and comic books, filling their lives with joy and laughter. Amal eagerly reached for his father's hand, knowing that it held treasures beyond his wildest dreams.

Meanwhile, Tessy and Sanjay approached the scene slowly, their footsteps heavy with uncertainty. Tessy silently urged Sanjay to go and speak with his father, despite his hesitance. With a gentle nudge from his mother, Sanjay reluctantly approached Aravind, who enveloped him in a warm hug and offered him special chocolates.

But as Tessy watched the exchange between father and sons, her heart grew heavy with conflicted emotions. When Amal interrupted to recount the events of the school day and the punishment Tessy had imposed on Aravind, Tessy's frustration boiled over.

Aravind, however, responded with understanding and reassurance, explaining to Amal that everything Tessy did was out of love for her children. He then turned to Tessy, extending a small welcome gesture, but Tessy's anger and resentment remained palpable.

Aravind approached Tessy with a heavy heart, explaining that his mother was bedridden and her greatest wish was to see her grandchildren. He requested Tessy to allow children to visit their grandmother for just three days.

Tessy, feeling irritated and tense, couldn't fathom the idea of sending her children away, even for a short time. Despite understanding Aravind's situation, she found it difficult to entertain his request.

Aravind sensed Tessy's irritation but continued to plead with her, emphasizing the importance of fulfilling his mother's wish. However, Tessy remained firm in her decision, stating that she couldn't send their children away under any circumstances.

As the church clock chimed 12:00 PM, Tessy reminded Aravind that their court-mandated hour was up, signalling the end of their discussion and their departure to pick up their sons. With a heavy heart, she called Sanjay and Amal to leave, the sorrow evident on Amal face as they bid their father farewell.

As they exited the church, the weight of unresolved emotions hung heavy in the air, leaving behind a sense of sorrow and longing for what could have been.

Part 7

FAREWELL DAY REVELATIONS

The year was April 11th 2008, and Dr. Paul's Engineering College, Tamil Nadu, nestled near Puducherry Union Territory, held a special place in the hearts of many. Puducherry name alone brought joy for various reasons, but one special reason stood out for the male students. The college was conveniently located near the serene enclave of Auroville, adding to its allure.

As one approached the college gates, a watchman dressed in crisp white attire diligently checked each person entering through the grand brown gates. At the entrance stood a majestic statue of the college founder, a reminder of the institution's rich history and legacy.

Inside the campus, the administrative office bustled with activity as staff members tended to their duties, while the accounts section meticulously handled financial matters. Beyond these buildings loomed the main academic building, a formidable structure rising nearly five floors high. Each floor housed a multitude of classrooms, including specialized labs for computer science, mechanical engineering, electrical engineering, and more.

To ensure proper airflow, the building boasted multi-layered windows that let in natural light and fresh air. In the rear of the building, an impressive auditorium stood tall, adorned with a water fountain designed to resemble a tree. With seating capacity for 2000 people spread across two floors, the auditorium served as a venue for various events and gatherings.

Today marked a significant occasion for the college – the farewell day for the 2004-2008 batch. Students from different engineering departments roamed the campus, capturing cherished moments with their friends as they prepared to bid farewell to their alma mater and embark on the next chapter of their lives.

In the bustling classroom of Class 204, final year Computer Science and Engineering students were engaged in various activities on their last day of class. Among these activities was a game called "We Want to Know What You Are." The rules were simple: students would pick a folded paper from a glass box containing their classmates' names, person stands in front of their peers, and answer questions posed by their friends.

Amidst the excitement, a girl picked a name from the glass box, revealing it to be Aravind. With a lively call, Aravind stepped onto the dais, exuding youthfulness and clad in traditional Tamil Nadu attire. His friends bombarded him with a barrage of questions, to which he responded with ease and humour.

However, amidst the clamour, Tessy, with her charming and overactive demeanour, took charge. She called for a pause in the questioning, declaring that she had a question of her own for Aravind.

Tessy, with her captivating presence, was the embodiment of beauty and grace. Her features were a symphony of perfection – light pink skin, her nose delicately sculpted, her eyes bright and expressive, and her curly hair cascading down like a waterfall of silk. Her body was neither too lean nor too plump; it was compact and perfect, exuding an aura of timeless beauty. Tessy was not just beautiful; she was enchanting from head to toe. Her voice, bold and melodic, could conquer hearts and command attention, adding another layer to her irresistible charm.

Aravind, on the other hand, was a study in contrasts. Tall and well-built, his physique was the result of years of dedication and hard work. His skin was a warm bronze, neither too dark nor too light, perfectly complementing his quiet demeanour. Aravind was a man of few words, his silence often misinterpreted as aloofness, but those who knew him understood it was simply his nature. He preferred observing the world rather than speaking out, finding comfort in his thoughts and the quiet strength they gave him.

Despite his impressive physical stature, Aravind was deeply intimidated by Tessy's vibrant presence. He admired her from a distance, his heart swelling with unspoken affection. Tessy's laughter was like music to his ears, her colourful personality brightening even the dullest of days. Aravind often found himself lost in thoughts of her, but the fear of rejection kept him from voicing his feelings. He worried that his average looks and reserved nature would never match up to Tessy's radiant beauty and bold demeanour.

Aravind stood nervously, his sports-built body betraying his anxiety with trembling legs. Despite his athletic nature, the prospect of the upcoming question from Tessy made him uneasy. With his artistic face, coloured in shades of brown, he nodded slightly as he met Tessy's sparking eyes.

Tessy, radiating beauty from head to toe, prepared to speak. Her lips, painted in a bold red, formed the question that Aravind anticipated. She adjusted her curly hair, causing her big earrings to catch the light and cast a glow on Aravind's face.

For the past four years, Aravind had harboured a one-sided love for Tessy, and now, as she prepared to ask her question, he eagerly awaited her words, hoping they would reveal her true feelings.

Confident in her posture, Tessy leaned forward, ready to ask Aravind the next question. Aravind braced himself, his shivering legs a stark contrast to Tessy's composed demeanour. As Tessy spoke, Aravind listened intently, knowing that his response would determine the course of their conversation.

As the room fell silent, all eyes turned to Tessy, and Aravind couldn't help but smile, his heart pounding with anticipation.

As Tessy posed her question, the classroom fell into a hushed anticipation. "Do you smoke?" she inquired, her gaze steady and unwavering. Aravind, with a quiet affirmation, admitted to his habit, prompting a collective reaction from the class. Tessy, undeterred by the uproar, silenced her classmates with a determined smile.

Refusing to be swayed, Tessy pressed on, her next question hanging in the air. "Who do you like very most in the college?"

she asked, her eyes locking with Aravind's. The room grew tense as everyone waited for his response, the silence deafening.

Suddenly, the tranquillity was shattered by the jarring ringtone of a cell phone. Gunasekaran, the class representative, urgently called out for the phone to be silenced, eager to maintain order. With all eyes on Aravind, he hesitated for a moment, his gaze fixed on Tessy's expectant face.

Then, breaking the silence, Aravind uttered a single phrase: "Unna than" – "It's you." The words hung in the air, a revelation that sent a wave of joy rippling through the classroom. As the college bell chimed, signalling the end of the day, the students erupted into cheers and applause.

Tessy, her heart brimming with happiness, met Aravind's gaze with a silent understanding. In that moment, amidst the cacophony of celebration, their eyes spoke volumes, conveying a shared sense of joy and affection that transcended words.

As the classroom emptied out, Aravind remained rooted in place, his expression a mixture of anticipation and uncertainty. Tessy, her cheeks flushed with a newfound blush, caught his eye, her radiant presence akin to that of an angel descending from the heavens. Draped in a Kerala traditional saree, she exuded an ethereal charm that captivated all who beheld her.

As their friends playfully teased and joked while leaving the class, Tessy approached Aravind, her voice soft but determined. She informed him of her plans to travel to Wayanad, Kerala, that evening, with a bus scheduled to depart at 8:30 PM. With her announcement made, Tessy gracefully exited the classroom, leaving Aravind standing alone, his emotions swirling within him.

Aravind remained in place, his mind consumed with thoughts of Tessy and the confession he had made moments ago. Amidst the flurry of activity, he stood in solitude, grappling with the weight of his feelings and the uncertainty of what the future held. As the echoes of the bustling classroom faded into the distance, Aravind found himself lost in contemplation, his heart yearning for the possibility of a love that transcended time and distance.

Part 8

JOURNEY OF HOPE

As the clock neared 7:55 PM, Aravind found himself racing against time, seated behind his friend Mugilan on a speeding bike. Mugilan, a student from the ECE (Electronics and Communication Engineering) branch, was an anomaly among his peers. Despite his distinct personality, he shared an unbreakable bond with Aravind, one that had been forged over years of shared experiences and unwavering loyalty. Mugilan was tall and lean, standing at six feet, with a lanky frame that earned him the affectionate nickname "Lizard" among friends, they navigated through the bustling streets of Puducherry, with Aravind's heart pounding in his chest with each passing second.

As they reached the iconic Muruga Theatre signal, bathed in the glow of its crimson light, Aravind's urgency grew palpable. He shouted to Mugilan, urging him to hasten their journey. With every countdown of the signal - 9, 8, 7... - Aravind's anxiety mounted, knowing that time was slipping away.

When the light finally turned green, Aravind's relief was palpable as Mugilan accelerated their bike forward. With determination,

Aravind guided Mugilan through a shortcut, bypassing the congested main road and heading towards the bus stand.

Despite the obstacles along the way, including the usual traffic snarls and winding streets, Aravind's determination never wavered. Finally, at 8:10 PM, they arrived at the Puducherry main bus stand, the bustling hub of travel connecting southern India.

With a sense of accomplishment, Aravind and Mugilan breathed a sigh of relief as they disembarked from the bike. Aravind's heart still raced with the adrenaline of their journey, but now, standing at the threshold of his departure, he felt a surge of anticipation for the journey ahead.

As Aravind made his way through the entrance of the Puducherry main bus stand, his eyes caught sight of Hotel Mass, renowned for its jug beer. Despite the tempting prospect, Aravind pressed on, passing by vendors selling flowers and snacks at the entrance gate.

Aravind hurried through the bustling bus stand; his mind consumed with thoughts of Tessy. He had promised to meet her, but as he passed by a CD shop, something caught his eye. The display boasted an array of CDs featuring songs by various music directors – Ilaiyaraaja hits, Harris Jayaraj hits, A.R. Rahman classics, and Yuvan Shankar Raja melodies.

Despite being in a hurry, Aravind felt a sudden urge to browse through the collection. He knew he should continue on his way to meet Tessy, but the allure of Yuvan Shankar Raja's soulful melodies was irresistible.

Aravind found himself drawn to the Yuvan melodies section. He scanned through the CDs, each one promising a collection of beautiful songs that could transport him to another world. The memories associated with Yuvan's music flooded his mind, reminding him of happier times and easing the tension in his heart.

Without thinking twice, Aravind grabbed a Yuvan melodies CD and hurried to the counter to make his purchase. As he handed over the money, With the CD in hand, Aravind rushed towards his destination.

Navigating through the rows of buses, Aravind finally located the Kerala state bus stand, where buses bound for various destinations in Kerala were lined up. With the clock ticking past 8:25 PM, Aravind felt a pang of uncertainty wash over him.

Suddenly, a gentle touch on his shoulder startled Aravind, causing him to turn around. There stood Tessy, her presence calming his nerves with a simple smile. Aravind couldn't help but return her smile, though he remained silent in her presence.

Aravind stood before Tessy, holding out a CD of Yuvan Shankar Raja melodies with a shy smile on his face. "I saw this and thought of you," he said, extending the gift towards her.

Tessy's eyes lit up with delight as she took the CD from Aravind's hands. "Yuvan is my favourite!" she exclaimed, her smile widening. "Thank you so much, Aravind."

Aravind's face brightened at Tessy's reaction, his cheeks flushed with a mix of happiness and nervousness. Despite the sweat forming on his brow in the night's humidity, he felt a sense of warmth fill his heart at the sight of Tessy's joy.

As they stood together under the dim lights, Aravind and Tessy shared a moment of connection, bonded by their love for music. The soft glow of the night enveloped them, casting a magical aura around their exchange.

Seeking clarity amidst the chaos, Aravind inquired about the departure time of the bus. Tessy's response confirmed his suspicions - the bus to Wayanad was scheduled to depart at 8:30 PM. With a nod of understanding, Aravind's gaze fell upon the red-coloured KSRTC bus, its destination boldly displayed in both English and Malayalam.

In that moment, amidst the hustle and bustle of the bus stand, Aravind felt a sense of reassurance wash over him, knowing that Tessy was by his side. With renewed determination, he prepared to embark on his journey to Wayanad, his heart filled with anticipation for the adventures that lay ahead.

As the bus prepared to embark on its journey, Tessy bid farewell to Aravind, her voice tinged with a hint of sadness. However, Aravind's unexpected request caught her off guard. With a furrowed brow, she questioned how he intended to join her without a ticket. Aravind, undeterred, assured her that he would find a way.

With the driver's impatient shout signalling the imminent departure, Tessy made her way onto the bus. Aravind, determined not to be left behind, sprinted after her and approached the bus conductor with a plea. However, the conductor regretfully informed him that there were no available seats, only the option to stand for the lengthy journey ahead.

Despite the discomfort of standing for 14 hours, Aravind resolved to join Tessy on the journey. As he entered the bus, Tessy couldn't help but smile at his determination, though she couldn't shake the feeling of concern for his well-being.

As the bus rumbled to life and began its journey, the soothing strains of old Malayalam songs filled the air. One by one, passengers succumbed to the lullaby of the music, drifting off into slumber. Yet, amidst the peaceful quietude of the bus, Aravind and Tessy's eyes met, silently communicating a connection that transcended words.

As the bus crossed the Kerala state border into the picturesque region of Wayanad, the landscape underwent a breathtaking transformation. Rolling hills adorned with lush greenery stretched as far as the eye could see, creating a mesmerizing panorama of natural beauty.

Entering Wayanad, the bus traversed through dense forests, where towering teakwood and rosewood trees lined the winding roads. Notices warning of elephant crossings and urging passengers not to disturb the wildlife served as reminders of the region's rich biodiversity.

Amidst the tranquil surroundings, deer grazed peacefully in the midst of the forest, their graceful movements adding to the allure of the scenery. With each passing mile, the bus navigated carefully through the forested terrain, the gentle morning breeze carrying with it the scent of wildflowers and earth.

Against this backdrop of natural splendour, the strains of old Kerala songs continued to fill the air, enhancing the sense of serenity and tranquillity. As the bus approached Sultan Bathery, a town nestled amidst the hills of Wayanad, Aravind found himself enraptured by the sheer beauty of the surroundings.

Turning to Tessy, he couldn't help but smile, his heart overflowing with appreciation for the beauty of both nature and his companion. In that moment, amidst the idyllic setting of Wayanad, Aravind felt an overwhelming sense of gratitude for the opportunity to experience such magnificence alongside Tessy.

As the bus conductor's voice echoed through the air, announcing the arrival at Sultan Bathery, Tessy wasted no time in making her way towards the exit. Aravind, albeit more slowly, followed suit, his movements deliberate as he observed the unfolding scene.

Stepping off the bus, Aravind was greeted by the breathtaking beauty of Sultan Bathery. The undulating roads snaking through the mountains painted a picture-perfect scene, enhanced by the light drizzle and the chill in the air. Despite the cold, Aravind found solace in Tessy's presence, knowing she was there to support him.

In the heart of the city, the towering clock machine indicated the time as 10 o'clock, its hands ticking steadily amidst the light rainfall. Tessy, mindful of Aravind's presence, apologized to him, though he seemed puzzled by her remorse. Yet, Tessy reiterated her apology, explaining that she couldn't engage with him further as she had relatives awaiting her.

With a sense of determination, Tessy moved away, leaving Aravind to ponder the sights and sounds of Sultan Bathery. Amidst the hustle and bustle of the bus stand, amidst the flurry of activity and the mingling of voices, Sanjay's attention was abruptly diverted by a notification on his trusty Nokia 5310 Xpress Music phone.

Reading Tessy's heartfelt message, expressing a desire to journey together in life, Aravind was overcome with emotion. In that moment, amidst the chaos of the bus stand, he couldn't contain his joy, letting out a triumphant shout that echoed through the air. With a newfound sense of purpose, Sanjay prepared to embark on his own journey, one filled with hope, love, and endless possibilities.

Part 9

ECHOES OF COMPASSION

September 21 2009, a Monday morning dawned upon Chennai's bustling Koyambedu bus stand, renowned as Asia's largest bus terminus and a vibrant hub of activity. Amidst the hustle and bustle of the market, where vendors peddled fresh fruits and vegetables, thousands of people traversed the vast expanse, each lost in their own world.

In the midst of this bustling scene, Aravind found himself at a bus terminus shop, requesting a water bottle from the shopkeeper. However, to his surprise, the shopkeeper charged him Rs. 25 for a bottle marked with an MRP of Rs. 20. When Aravind questioned the discrepancy, the shopkeeper's response was curt and dismissive, a stark reminder of the harsh realities of urban life.

As Aravind begrudgingly handed over the extra money for the water bottle, his attention was diverted by the arrival of a Kerala-bound bus. Stepping out from the bus, carrying a large travel bag and wearing a sombre expression, was Tessy. Aravind's heart sank as he observed Tessy's distress, her tears betraying the turmoil within.

Concerned for Tessy, Aravind approached her with trepidation, gently inquiring about the cause of her distress. Tessy, her voice choked with emotion, struggled to articulate her anguish. Aravind, feeling a pang of helplessness, attempted to comfort Tessy, urging her to compose herself in the midst of the public space.

As Tessy's tears continued to flow, Aravind couldn't help but feel a sense of shame at his inability to alleviate her suffering. In that moment, amidst the chaos of the bus stand, Aravind realized the profound impact of human connection and the importance of empathy in navigating life's trials and tribulations.

In a gesture of kindness and concern, Aravind led Tessy to a cozy bamboo restaurant nestled amidst the vibrant streets of Kodambakkam. Known for its association with the Kollywood film industry, Kodambakkam exuded a unique charm, with movie studios dotting its landscape. The bamboo restaurant, situated on the rooftop of a five-story building, offered a serene escape from the bustling city below.

As Aravind and Tessy stepped into the restaurant, they were greeted warmly by the staff, who directed them to a private dining third hut. Tessy found solace in the natural ambiance of the restaurant, constructed entirely of bamboo sticks, with each hut providing a sense of privacy and tranquillity. Sitting down in the dining hut, Tessy felt a wave of calm wash over her.

Observing Tessy's newfound serenity, Aravind gently broached the subject of her distress, prompting Tessy to open up about her struggles. Over the past month, Tessy had endured pressure from her father to marry according to his wishes, despite her love for Aravind. Feeling suffocated by her father's expectations, Tessy had made the difficult decision to leave home in search of independence and freedom.

Listening intently to Tessy's plight, Aravind reached out and gently touched her hand, offering words of reassurance and hope. Encouraging Tessy to indulge in the delicious offerings of the restaurant, Aravind sought to lift her spirits amidst the turmoil. As they savoured their meal together, Tessy couldn't help but notice the changes in Aravind's appearance, remarking on his newfound confidence and sophistication.

In turn, Aravind acknowledged Tessy's transformation, admiring her newfound sense of style and grace. Amidst the tranquil setting of the restaurant, Tessy and Aravind found comfort in each other's company, their shared history and unwavering bond serving as a source of strength amidst life's uncertainties.

Part 10

WHISPERS IN THE NIGHT

As Aravind gracefully mounted his beloved Royal Enfield, Tessy couldn't help but admire the sight before her. The vintage black bike seemed to be an extension of Aravind himself, exuding an air of confidence and rugged charm. With a swift kick, Aravind ignited the engine, its powerful roar filling the air as Tessy watched in awe.

However, their peaceful moment was abruptly interrupted by the intrusion of a dishevelled beggar, whose loud demands startled Tessy. In a protective gesture, Aravind swiftly intervened, firmly dismissing the beggar with a commanding presence. Tessy, grateful for Aravind's swift action, felt a sense of reassurance wash over her as she settled onto the back of the bike.

As they embarked on their journey, Tessy shared some exciting news with Aravind, she had requested a transfer to Chennai from her current job at Kochi, EI bound Systems Pvt Limited, and the HR manager had approved it after understanding her situation.

Tessy felt relieved and happy about the opportunity to work in Chennai's bustling OMR area.

As they navigated through the chaotic streets of Chennai, Tessy couldn't help but feel the sting of the hot and dusty air against her skin. Despite the discomfort, she found solace in Aravind's reassuring presence, wrapping her arms around him in a tight embrace.

In that fleeting moment, as they rode through the bustling cityscape, Tessy and Aravind found comfort in each other's company, their shared journey serving as a testament to their unwavering bond amidst life's trials and tribulations.

As Aravind pulled up in front of Professor Catherine Ladies Hostel, Tessy's heart weighed heavy with the thought of parting ways, even if only for a short while. Sitting astride the bike, Tessy couldn't help but express her longing to explore the world with Aravind by her side. With a resolve in her voice, she announced her decision to join the hostel the following day, determined to navigate the challenges ahead with Aravind's love and support.

As they embarked on their ride along the scenic East Coast Road, Tessy found herself captivated by the mesmerizing beauty of the sea waves crashing against the shore. Overwhelmed by the serenity of the moment, Tessy wrapped her arms around Aravind, seeking solace in his embrace. Their journey through the quaint streets of Uthandi (ECR Tollgate) led them to the tranquil shores of the sea.

With a sense of childlike joy, Tessy dipped her feet into the cool, refreshing waters of the sea, relishing the feeling of freedom and liberation it brought her. Meanwhile, Aravind sat in quiet contemplation, his mind racing with thoughts of the future and the challenges that lay ahead.

Despite the uncertainty that loomed on the horizon, Aravind found solace in the knowledge that Tessy's unwavering love and determination would guide them through any storm. As they sat by the sea, enveloped in the comforting embrace of each other's presence, Aravind silently vowed to do everything in his power to ensure Tessy's happiness and safety, come what may.

As evening descended upon them, Aravind and Tessy arrived at the opulent apartment complex in Perungudi, located along the bustling OMR, near the tollgate. Aravind, with a sense of pride, led Tessy to the apartment where he resided with his friends. Inside the lift, amidst the soft hum of its ascent, Aravind couldn't resist asking Tessy about the unwavering trust she placed in him. Tessy's smile was her only response, her faith in Aravind as inexplicable to her as it was genuine.

Upon reaching the fourth floor, Aravind guided Tessy to the apartment entrance. A somewhat unconventional greeting awaited them as Arun, one of Aravind's friends, answered the door, his casual attire reflecting the relaxed atmosphere of the apartment. As Arun welcomed them inside, Tessy couldn't help but notice the lived-in feel of the space, a testament to the camaraderie shared among its occupants.

Stepping into the living area, Tessy's eyes fell upon the room where Aravind and Aravind's friend, resided. As Aravind and Arun conversed in the living area, Tessy busied herself in the room, freshening up after their journey. Arun, sensing Aravind's apprehension, sought permission to go out for his friend's room today night, hinting at a surprise to lift Aravind's spirits. Arun moves to his friend's home and Aravind locked the door.

Displeased with the disorderliness of the space, Tessy took it upon herself to rectify the situation, insisting that Aravind wait outside while she tidied up. With meticulous care and attention to detail, Tessy transformed the room into a welcoming haven, her actions reflecting her unwavering commitment to creating a comfortable environment for Aravind.

Aravind, though initially apprehensive about inviting Tessy into his living quarters, couldn't help but feel a sense of admiration and gratitude for her unwavering support and willingness to make their temporary home feel like their own. As Tessy emerged from the room, a radiant smile gracing her features, Aravind knew that he was truly blessed to have her by his side. Together, they embarked on this new chapter of their journey, their bond stronger than ever before.

Just as Aravind was beginning to relax, the doorbell chimed, causing him to tense up once again. Aravind opened the door anxiously and its food delivery boy, the food was ordered by his friend Arun, Aravind couldn't help but feel curious as he accepted the delivery of a large parcel of food.

With the food in hand, Aravind made his way to the room where Tessy was getting ready. As he entered and locked the door, he found Tessy emerging from the bathroom, clad in a comfortable nightwear ensemble—a sleeveless t-shirt adorned with the word "Happy" and half trousers. The sight of Tessy, with her easy smile and relaxed demeanour, instantly lifted Aravind's spirits, reminding him of the simple joy of being together.

Tessy was famished, and as Aravind brought her food, she couldn't wait to dig in. Aravind watched her eat, his eyes lingering on her hair, lips, and every movement. He found himself admiring the way she ate, wishing he could be the food that crossed her lips.

After finishing her meal, Tessy noticed that Aravind hadn't eaten. Concerned, she asked him why, but before she could finish, Aravind whispered in her ear, confessing that he couldn't control himself. He pulled her into a tight hug, his hands exploring every inch of her body.

Tessy was speechless as Aravind's touch ignited a fire within her. She could feel his desire, and despite her confusion, she found herself responding to his embrace. Aravind seemed to lose control, his senses overwhelmed by Tessy's scent and presence.

Aravind's passion seemed to know no bounds as he embraced Tessy, his touch becoming more intense with each passing moment. Tessy captivated and overwhelmed by Aravind's fervour.

As the night wore on, Aravind eventually fell asleep in Tessy's lap, his grip on her loosening as he drifted off into slumber. Tessy looked down at him, smiling softly at the sight of her Aravind sleeping so peacefully.

Throughout the night, Tessy spoke to Aravind about her fears, her hopes, and her dreams. Aravind slept like a baby; his worries temporarily forgotten in the comfort of Tessy's presence.

In the quiet of the night, Tessy found solace in Aravind's embrace, cherishing the moment of intimacy and connection they shared. And as the first light of dawn broke through the window, Tessy knew that despite their struggles, they would find a way to overcome their challenges together.

Part 11

RAINY DAY RESILIENCE

On a rainy Monday morning, October 22, 2009, Tessy woke up in her room at Professor Catherine Ladies Hostel feeling unwell. The rain tapping against the windowpane seemed to exacerbate her headache and nausea. Rushing to the bathroom, she was plagued by bouts of vomiting for the next couple of hours, leaving her exhausted and drained.

Meanwhile, Aravind was engrossed in a crucial conference at his office in Ascends Infotainment IT Park. Mr. Sunil Kethu, their manager, was emphasizing the importance of a bank project, stressing its significant value for the company. Aravind was fully focused on the meeting, but his phone buzzed incessantly. Glancing at the caller ID, he saw that it was Tessy, but he couldn't afford to be distracted and ignored the call.

As the meeting progressed, Aravind's team leader, Mr. Mohanraju, discussed strategies for efficiently delivering results. Despite his curiosity about Tessy's call, Aravind remained attentive to the discussion and refrained from answering.

After the meeting concluded around noon, Aravind returned to his cabin for a break. His colleague Deepika, who sat in the adjacent cubicle, remarked on the new project and predicted that they would be sent onsite to the United Kingdom within three years. Aravind smiled at the thought but couldn't shake off his concern for Tessy.

Finally, taking a moment to himself, Aravind decided to call Tessy back. He dialled her number, hoping to find out why she had been trying to reach him.

Tessy, feeling tired and unwell after a long bout of vomiting, finally managed to speak to Aravind. She explained her condition, her voice betraying her exhaustion. Aravind listened attentively; his concern evident in his voice as he asked her how she was feeling.

"I'm somewhat okay now," Tessy replied weakly, "but I'm still feeling sick. Can you come?"

Aravind hesitated, explaining that he had an important meeting for a new project scheduled for the afternoon. "This project is like a dream for me, Tessy," he said, his tone filled with enthusiasm. "But I'll come by evening. You just focus on getting better."

Understanding Aravind's commitment to his work, Tessy assured him that she would manage. "Take care, Aravind," she said softly. "I'll drink some hot water, Bread and take rest. You come in the evening."

Aravind nodded, his care for Tessy evident in his voice. "Make sure you take care of yourself, Tessy. I'll come and pick you up in the evening." With that, he hung up, determined to finish his work so he could be there for Tessy when she needed him.

In the evening at 7:00 pm, Aravind waited anxiously for Tessy outside the hostel. When she finally emerged, she looked exhausted and worn out. Despite her fatigue, she managed a smile for Aravind, who immediately noticed her condition and asked her what had happened, his heart filled with concern and love.

Tessy replied weakly, "I'm okay, just tired," but Aravind could see through her facade. He insisted they go to the hospital, gently but firmly leading her to his bike. They reached a nearby small clinic named Doctor M. Vishnu Priya's clinic.

Part 12

FACING THE FUTURE

*I*nside the clinic, Aravind supported Tessy as they waited for the doctor. While waiting, Aravind noticed a baby wearing a stethoscope, playing happily. His interest piqued, Aravind watched the baby closely, a flicker of doubt crossing his mind. Could Tessy be pregnant?

As they waited for the doctor, Aravind's mind raced with thoughts about their future. If Tessy was indeed pregnant, it would change everything for them. But regardless of the outcome, Aravind was determined to support Tessy through whatever challenges they faced.

Aravind and Tessy entered the doctor's room, feeling anxious and uncertain about Tessy's health. As they waited for the previous patient to leave, they exchanged worried glances, both dreading what the doctor might say.

The doctor, a matured-aged woman with a warm smile and short hair, welcomed them into her clinic. Tessy explained her physical symptoms while Aravind listened attentively, his heart pounding with fear and anticipation.

After examining Tessy thoroughly, the doctor confirmed their worst fear: Tessy was pregnant. The news hit them like a ton of bricks, leaving them speechless and overwhelmed with emotions. Aravind and Tessy looked at each other, their eyes filled with fear and uncertainty about the future.

The doctor reassured them, explaining that pregnancy symptoms were common and that they would need to come back the next morning for further tests to confirm. In the meantime, she prescribed some medications to alleviate Tessy's discomfort.

Leaving the clinic, Aravind held Tessy's hand tightly, offering her silent support as they processed the shocking news. They knew their lives were about to change drastically, but they also knew they would face whatever challenges came their way together.

Aravind remained silent as he bought the prescribed medicines for Tessy. Dropping her off at the hostel, he didn't utter a single word about the pregnancy. Instead, he reassured her, telling Tessy not to overthink and promising that they would do all the necessary tests to confirm everything.

"Before that, don't be afraid," Aravind said gently.

Tessy felt confused by Aravind's silence on the matter. She walked slowly into the hostel, her mind swirling with questions about why he hadn't asked anything about the pregnancy. Despite her confusion, she trusted Aravind's words and decided to take his advice to rest.

Aravind sat alone in the tea shop near the Perungudi traffic light junction. The aroma of tea and the sound of vehicles passing by filled the air as he smoked, lost in his thoughts. He thought about Tessy's pregnancy and what it meant for their future.

The streetlights outside flickered as Aravind contemplated the sudden turn of events. He wondered how he would manage everything, from supporting Tessy to taking care of their child, if indeed she was pregnant.

As he sipped his tea, Aravind's mind raced with questions and uncertainties, but he was determined to face whatever challenges lay ahead.

Aravind arrived at Tessy's hostel early the next morning. Tessy, dressed in her formal attire for the office, came out to meet him. As they rode on Aravind's bike, Tessy broke the silence, expressing her desire to abort the child to prioritize Aravind. Aravind's eyes welled up with tears as he stopped the bike on the side of the road.

With a heavy heart, Aravind tried to convey to Tessy the importance of the child to him. He explained how much he wanted their baby and how he couldn't bear the thought of not having it. Tessy was taken aback by Aravind's response, realizing the depth of his feelings.

Aravind wiped away his tears and resumed riding. They reached the hospital, where the doctor confirmed Tessy's pregnancy. Tessy looked at Aravind, her eyes reflecting a mix of emotions - surprise, concern, and a hint of relief.

Aravind held Tessy's hand tightly, silently promising to support her through whatever decision they made together. As they left the hospital, the weight of the situation hung heavy in the air, but Aravind and Tessy knew they would face it together, no matter what.

Part 13

NEWLY-WEDS ON THE ROAD

On November 5th 2009, a Tuesday morning, Aravind and Tessy headed to the registrar office in Guindy, Chennai. Located near the governor's office and behind Anna University, the place was always bustling with people completing various legal formalities.

Aravind was eagerly awaiting the registration of their marriage. Tessy arrived wearing a beautiful green silk saree, looking radiant like an angel. Aravind felt a sense of hope seeing her.

As they waited for their turn, Aravind's college friend Mugilan informed him of Tessy's arrival. Aravind greeted Tessy with a smile, and she returned it, her eyes asking him how she looked. Aravind assured her she looked great.

Tessy and Aravind engaged in conversation while Mugilan went to check the registration timing. Tessy asked Aravind why he hadn't told his parents about their marriage plans. Aravind explained that he wanted to share the news with my parents in a joyful manner rather than out of fear, I am not in a position to call my parents, and I don't want too either.

Diverting the topic, Tessy complimented Aravind on his appearance. Mugilan then called them for their registration. Tessy held Aravind's hand tightly as they entered the registrar's office.

After completing the necessary procedures, they exchanged flower garlands as a symbol of their marriage. Tessy and Aravind were filled with happiness as they officially became husband and wife.

Aravind and Tessy felt relieved after their marriage registration and thanked Mugilan for his support. Mugilan inquired about their accommodation, and Aravind mentioned that he had already arranged a house in Family nest Apartments in Neelankarai, which is located near the starting point of ECR and close to the East Coast Sea. Gopinath, the marriage arranger, came to collect his brokerage fees, and Mugilan paid him with the money Aravind provided.

Mugilan then handed over his car key to Aravind, telling him to enjoy the day as it was his special day. He promised to return the key the next day. Aravind and Tessy happily got into the car and started their journey together.

Tessy smiled at Aravind as he drove the car. Curious about why Aravind hadn't informed his parents about their marriage, Tessy asked him. Aravind, still in a happy mood, replied, "I am just enjoying the moment. Let's not worry about anything else right now."

As they continued driving along ECR, they noticed a green distance board indicating Puducherry was 133 kilometres away. Suddenly, Aravind made an impromptu decision and said to

Tessy, "Let's go to Puducherry for a little getaway to celebrate our marriage."

Excited by the idea, Tessy readily agreed. They continued their journey towards Puducherry, enjoying the scenic beauty along the way. The cool breeze from the sea and the anticipation of their spontaneous trip filled the car.

After a couple of hours, they reached Puducherry and decided to explore the French Quarter first. They walked along the charming streets, admiring the colonial architecture and enjoying the relaxed atmosphere. They stopped by a cozy café and had some delicious French pastries and coffee.

Next, they visited the famous Promenade Beach and took a romantic stroll along the shore, feeling the gentle touch of the waves on their feet. They clicked some memorable pictures to cherish the moment forever.

As the evening approached, they decided to visit Auroville. They were mesmerized by the serene surroundings and spent some quiet time meditating in the Matrimandir.

After a day filled with adventure and joy, Aravind and Tessy returned to Chennai, feeling even more connected and in love. It was a trip they would always remember as the beginning of their beautiful journey together.

Part 14

BEARING LIFE

Tessy sat in a chair in the waiting area of Sandhiya Hospital, a renowned facility known for its expertise in pregnancy care. It was bustling with activity, filled with pregnant women accompanied by their husbands or parents. Tessy couldn't help but notice the care and support these women received from their loved ones.

Feeling a pang of loneliness, Tessy realized that she was alone. She was seven to eight months pregnant and waiting for her regular checkup. She watched as other women happily embraced the journey of pregnancy, despite the discomfort it brought.

Sandhiya Hospital was located near Perungudi and stood tall as a four-floor building. Tessy patiently waited on the ground floor for her turn. Suddenly, a white-clad assistant called out her name. Tessy acknowledged and followed the assistant to the doctor's room.

Inside, she met Doctor S. Shilpa, a skilled gynaecologist with MBBS and MD qualifications. Doctor Shilpa greeted Tessy warmly and invited her to sit down. Tessy felt a sense of comfort as she began her checkup, knowing she was in good hands with Doctor Shilpa, Doctor Shilpa asked Tessy about her health and how she was feeling, inquiring about any symptoms she might be experiencing. Tessy explained that overall, she was fine, but sometimes felt irritated, though she considered it manageable. The doctor then asked if Tessy had completed her regular scans and blood tests.

Tessy replied that she had just finished them the day before. Doctor Shilpa requested Tessy's hospital report chart, which Tessy promptly handed over. The doctor entered the details into the computer and reviewed the reports. She then informed Tessy that everything looked fine with the baby, but she needed to take care of herself as well. Tessy's haemoglobin levels were borderline, so the doctor advised her to continue her medications properly.

Understanding the importance of her own health for the baby's well-being, Tessy nodded in agreement. Doctor Shilpa emphasized that while the baby's health was crucial, the mother's health was equally important. Tessy smiled and promised to follow the doctor's advice. Before leaving, Tessy asked why she needed to come back in two weeks when monthly check-ups were the norm.

Doctor Shilpa explained that since the baby was due soon, it was crucial to monitor Tessy's health more closely. She informed Tessy that from now on, check-ups every two weeks were necessary to ensure everything was progressing smoothly. Tessy understood the significance and thanked the doctor before leaving the room.

Tessy travelled in a local cab, the summer heat bearing down on her. She called her husband Aravind, who was busy in his office working on data collection and generating reports for his team leader. Aravind smiled as he answered the call, eager to hear about Tessy's doctor's appointment.

Tessy simply replied that the doctor said everything was fine. Aravind sensed Tessy's tension and reassured her, expressing his love and understanding. He explained that his dedication to his work was for their future, especially their children's education and their dream of living in London. Tessy felt relieved hearing Aravind's words, knowing his hard work was for their family's well-being.

As Tessy's cab stopped behind traffic on OMR, Aravind continued to reassure her, expressing his love and dedication to their family. Tessy appreciated his support but asked him not to give reasons for her baby's delivery when he called.

Approaching her office, Tessy told Aravind that she missed him during her doctor's appointments. Aravind wanted to continue the conversation romantically, but Tessy reminded him she was near her office and promised to call him later, Tessy paid the cab driver and entered her office El bound Systems private limited.

Part 15

WOMEN'S REBIRTH

MAY 20TH 2010

Tessy gripped Aravind's fingers tightly as she felt the intense labor pains surging through her body. They were in the operation theatre, surrounded by doctors and medical staff. Doctor Shilpa, along with two other doctors, was leading the process to deliver the baby without surgery, trying their best to ensure a smooth delivery for Tessy and the baby.

Aravind stood by Tessy's side, holding her hand firmly, offering words of encouragement and support as she endured the pain. Tessy's face was contorted with discomfort, but she remained determined to bring their child into the world.

Doctor Shilpa and her team worked swiftly and efficiently, carefully monitoring Tessy's condition and the progress of the labor. They adjusted their approach as needed, using various techniques to facilitate the delivery and ensure the safety of both mother and baby.

Despite the challenges and the intensity of the moment, Tessy remained remarkably calm, trusting in the expertise of the medical team and drawing strength from Aravind's presence beside her.

As Tessy's labor progressed, the doctors noticed that she was struggling to push the baby out effectively. Concerned about the situation, Doctor Shilpa and her team decided to administer medication to help facilitate the birth.

Aravind was asked to wait outside the operation theatre as the doctors felt his discomfort might affect Tessy's focus during the procedure. Despite Tessy's insistence that she wanted him by her side, the doctors insisted that Aravind wait outside for the time being. With a heavy heart, Aravind reluctantly complied, silently praying for Tessy and their unborn child.

Inside the theatre, Tessy was determined to do whatever it took to bring their baby into the world safely. The doctors encouraged her to push with all her strength, but despite her efforts, the baby seemed reluctant to make an appearance.

As time passed and Tessy grew tired, the doctors decided to intervene further. They prepared to administer medication to help stimulate the birth process. Doctor Shilpa explained to Tessy the purpose of the medication and assured her that it would help the baby come out more quickly.

Tessy nodded in understanding; her determination unwavering despite her exhaustion. She braced herself as the doctors administered the medication. Aravind, waiting anxiously outside, tried to keep his composure as he imagined the scene unfolding in the operation theatre.

As Tessy's labor progressed, Doctor Shilpa decided to administer medication to speed up the delivery of the baby. However, things took a turn for the worse when the placenta broke, and water started leaking from it. The doctors became alarmed as they realized the urgency of the situation.

Concerned for both Tessy and the baby's safety, the doctors quickly made the decision to proceed with an emergency caesarean section. They explained the situation to Tessy, who felt hopeless and desperately wanted to speak with her husband, Aravind.

Aravind rushed into the room as soon as he was called, his heart sinking at the sight of Tessy's tears. But he knew he had to stay strong for her. After hearing the situation from the doctors, Aravind reassured Tessy that everything would be alright. He held her tightly, offering her comfort and strength in her moment of distress.

As the medical team prepared to transfer Tessy to the Advanced operation theatre, she expressed her desire to speak with her mother. Aravind quickly dialled her mother's number and handed the phone to Tessy. But to Tessy's dismay, her mother didn't want to hear her voice and abruptly ended the call. The rejection only added to Tessy's pain, and she cried even harder.

Aravind held Tessy close, whispering words of encouragement and love. He didn't let her see the fear that gripped his own heart as they prepared for the surgery. With Aravind's support, Tessy was wheeled into the operation theatre, where Doctor Shilpa and the medical team were ready to begin the procedure.

The operation commenced, and Aravind could do nothing but wait anxiously outside the theatre, his prayers fervent as he pleaded with God for the safety of both Tessy and their baby.

Finally, after what felt like an eternity, the sound of a baby crying filled the air. Aravind's heart swelled with relief and joy as he heard the precious sound. Tears of gratitude streamed down his face as he thanked God for answering his prayers.

Doctor Shilpa emerged from the theatre with a smile, delivering the news that both Tessy and the baby were safe. Aravind's eyes filled with tears of joy as he rushed to Tessy's side, overwhelmed with emotion as he held his newborn boy child for the first time. Despite the challenges they faced, their love had triumphed, and their family was now complete.

As Aravind waited to speak with Doctor Shilpa about Tessy's discharge from the hospital, he noticed a married couple coming out of the doctor's room, their faces filled with tears. Aravind, who had a friendly rapport with Doctor Shilpa, approached her and inquired about the couple's situation.

With a heavy heart, Doctor Shilpa explained that the couple had lost their first baby due to lack of proper care, despite waiting for a year to conceive. Now, they were facing difficulties in conceiving again. Aravind listened intently to the doctor's words, struck by the poignant reminder of the fragility of life and the importance of proper care during pregnancy and childbirth.

Doctor Shilpa then reassured Aravind that Tessy was doing well and would be discharged from the hospital in a couple of days after, her stitches were removed latterly. Aravind thanked the doctor for her care and guidance, realizing the importance of being vigilant and attentive throughout Tessy's pregnancy and beyond.

With a newfound sense of responsibility and gratitude, Aravind made his way to Tessy's room. He couldn't wait to see her and their newborn baby, cherishing the precious moments they would share as a family.

Part 16

FROM SMILES TO CRIES

AUGUST 8TH 2010

As the baby naming function approached, excitement filled the air in Aravind and Tessy's apartment. A colourful banner announcing the occasion was proudly displayed, catching the attention of all the residents. The function hall, located in the centre of the apartment complex, was adorned with vibrant chairs, creating a festive atmosphere.

Aravind's friend Mugilan, along with his office colleagues, had taken charge of organizing the event. They worked tirelessly to ensure everything was set up perfectly. Aravind, with his energetic demeanour, couldn't help but shout out to Mugilan about the number of balloons. Mugilan, with a smile on his face, reassured Aravind that the room was already filled with balloons of various colours, including white and pink.

In the kitchen, Jabbar Bhai was busy preparing delicious biryani for the guests. Aravind popped in to check on the progress, and

Jabbar Bhai confidently informed him that the biryani was in full swing and ready to delight the guests.

Aravind, dressed casually in shorts and a t-shirt, greeted the arriving guests as they started to pour into the function hall. Among them were Aravind's office friends, college buddies, and Tessy's friends as well. As the guests mingled and enjoyed the lively atmosphere, Aravind excused himself to his apartment to dress more formally for the occasion. He wanted everything to be perfect for Tessy and their newborn baby's special day.

Aravind crossed the bustling apartment complex, passing by the towering buildings, each consisting of 16 floors. He reached Block A, where the entrance was surrounded by lush greenery. The apartment blocks were distinguished by different colours, and Block A was painted in a dark green hue.

Aravind stepped into the lift and pressed the button for the 8th floor. As the lift ascended, he couldn't shake off the sound of the baby's cries echoing in his mind.

Upon reaching their 2BHK home on the 8th floor, Aravind rang the doorbell. Tessy, still in her nightwear, opened the door with a tired smile. Aravind quickly noticed the baby's crying and hurried to the bathroom, asking Tessy why she had left him alone.

Tessy tried to explain, but Aravind was already comforting the baby, soothing him with gentle words. Tessy sighed, realizing Aravind's concern, and handed the baby to him.

Aravind urged Tessy to get ready as time was running out. Tessy reluctantly agreed, taking the baby from Aravind's arms. Aravind left the room to get ready himself, leaving Tessy to tend to their crying child.

As the clock struck 6:00 PM, Aravind was getting ready in his black suit, looking every bit the epitome of elegance and style. The suit accentuated his already great personality, giving him a sophisticated aura.

Meanwhile, Tessy was getting ready in a stunning black saree adorned with small white stones that shimmered under the evening lights. The saree perfectly complemented her beauty, enhancing her grace and charm but Tessy looks little fat.

Their son looked equally handsome in a white silky shirt paired with silky Trouser. His chubby cheeks and bright eyes added to his adorable appearance, making him the centre of attention wherever he went.

Aravind lifted their son into his arms, holding him close to his chest, while holding Tessy's hand with his free hand. Together, they made their way towards the function hall, where their friends and family eagerly awaited their arrival.

As they entered the hall, they were greeted with warm smiles and cheerful greetings. Tessy couldn't help but feel a surge of happiness as she looked around at the familiar faces, surrounded by the love and support of their loved ones.

As Aravind and Tessy stood on the stage, surrounded by colourful balloons, Tessy felt a surge of nervousness. Holding Aravind's hand tightly, she looked out at the crowd, feeling somewhat overwhelmed by the attention.

Sensing Tessy's discomfort, Aravind gently reassured her, suggesting that she take a seat. Tessy nodded gratefully, finding relief in the idea of sitting down amidst the bustling crowd.

Their friends and family eagerly asked about the baby's name, prompting Aravind to call over Mugilan, their close friend who was helping in all his life. Aravind whispered the baby's name into Mugilan's ear, instructing him to call out the name through their child's ears first.

Moved by the gesture, Mugilan smiled and nodded in understanding. With tears welling up in his eyes, he stepped forward and called out the baby's name in baby's ears, "Sanjay, Sanjay, Sanjay," three times. The baby's face lit up with a radiant smile, which seemed to illuminate the room. Mugilan's voice echoed through the space as he repeated the name once more, "Sanjay," in front of everyone, his heart filled with joy and gratitude.

Tessy, feeling dizzy from the noise of the crowd, leaned back in her chair, finding solace in the familiar sound of Mugilan's voice. Aravind stood by her side, offering her comfort and support as they welcomed their little one into the world with tears of joy and gratitude.

After the naming ceremony, everyone moved to the dining area where Aravind had arranged a sumptuous feast. The aroma of the chicken biryani filled the air, making everyone's mouth water. Alongside the biryani, there were delicious accompaniments like bread halwa and various Flavors of ice cream.

Jabbar and his workers served the food with great enthusiasm, ensuring everyone got their fill. The guests, excited and hungry, rushed to grab their plates and fill them with the mouth-watering dishes. Smiles lit up their faces as they indulged in the flavourful biryani.

Aravind, with a caring demeanour, made sure everyone was comfortable and enjoying the meal. Meanwhile, Tessy started to feel calmer as the hustle and bustle of the function hall began to empty out.

As the dinner progressed, Aravind noticed Tessy's relaxed state and took the opportunity to feed her himself. It was a tender moment, a symbol of their love and care for each other amidst the joyous celebrations.

As the guests savoured every bite of the delicious meal, the atmosphere was filled with laughter, chatter, and contentment. It was a heartwarming evening, one that Aravind and Tessy would cherish forever.

In the quiet aftermath of the celebration, Aravind and Tessy sat in the empty function hall. The echo of the earlier festivities had faded, leaving behind a tranquil silence. The guests had all departed, and the couple now found themselves alone amidst the decorations and remnants of the event.

Aravind had just given some money to Mugilan, instructing him to settle the payment to Jabbar Bhai for the biryani. As he turned back to Tessy, concern etched on his face, he asked, "Tessy, what's been going on with your health? You seemed a bit off today."

Tessy sighed, her eyes reflecting the weight of her worries. "I've been feeling a bit nervousness in the crowded place. I didn't want to ruin the event by talking about it now. We can discuss it later."

Their conversation was interrupted by the arrival of the watchman, who approached Aravind with a sense of urgency. "Sir, there are two people waiting to see you outside."

Aravind furrowed his brow in curiosity. "Who are they?"

The watchman hesitated. "Wait, sir. I'll call them in."

Moments later, two figures entered the function hall. As soon as Aravind saw them, he froze. His heart pounded in his chest, and tears welled up in his eyes. "Father, Mother," he whispered, barely able to believe his eyes. The dam of emotion burst, and he cried out loud, rushing towards them.

Aravind embraced his parents, the weight of his hidden marriage pressing heavily on his heart. "Mom, Dad, I did wrong. I don't know how to tell you. It all happened so suddenly with fear I'm fail to tell you my marriage, my child birth," he sobbed, his words tumbling out in a desperate plea for forgiveness.

His father, Ravivaruman, stood silently, his face a mask of stern disapproval. His mother, Pallavi, cried uncontrollably, her tears mirroring Aravind's. "How could you do all this without fearless?" Pallavi's voice was choked with emotion.

Aravind's cries grew louder as he fell to his knees, clutching his mother's hand. "Please, Mom, forgive me. I was scared and didn't know how to tell you. It was never my intention to hurt you."

Pallavi's tears continued to flow, but she turned her face away, unable to bear the sight of her son's anguish. Ravivaruman, his expression hardening, placed a hand on Pallavi's shoulder, guiding her away.

"We're leaving," Ravivaruman said quietly, his voice tinged with frustration and sorrow. "From this moment on, we are dead to you. Do not follow us."

Aravind's world shattered. He watched in horror as his parents walked away, their backs turned to him, each step echoing with finality. He scrambled to his feet, reaching out in a desperate attempt to stop them. "No, please, don't go! I'm sorry! Please forgive me!"

But his cries fell on deaf ears. Ravivaruman and Pallavi continued their slow, heart-wrenching walk out of the function hall, leaving Aravind to collapse on the ground, his body wracked with sobs. Tessy rushed to his side, her own eyes filled with tears as she held him, trying to offer comfort amidst the storm of his grief.

Aravind's cries echoed through the empty hall, a poignant reminder of the consequences of his actions. The love and acceptance he yearned for seemed more distant than ever, leaving him to grapple with the overwhelming pain of his parents' rejection.

Part 17

DISPARITY IN RECOGNITION

DECEMBER 6TH 2012

Aravind and his team members gathered in the conference hall for a crucial meeting led by Priya Sharma, the senior manager. Priya Sharma, a 40-year-old woman with a bold personality, wore a dark sky-blue soft saree paired with a half-sleeved jacket and stylish sunglasses. As the meeting commenced, Priya Sharma addressed the team, explaining the bugs and issues reported by the client.

With a commanding tone, Priya Sharma emphasized the need to minimize errors and improve the product's functionality. Aravind, known for his expertise in product design and excellent Java coding skills, listened attentively as Priya Sharma directed him to focus on resolving the bugs.

Throughout the meeting, Priya Sharma's authoritative presence and clear instructions motivated the team to work efficiently.

She assured Aravind and his colleagues that they would receive messages about their performance appraisals by the evening.

Aravind left the conference hall feeling determined to address the issues raised by the client. He understood the importance of Priya Sharma's guidance and was eager to implement her suggestions to improve the product's quality. As the evening approached, the anticipation of a positive appraisal motivated Aravind and his team to work diligently to meet the client's expectations.

Feeling disappointed and puzzled, Aravind checked his email at 4:00 PM to find out about the hike in his salary. To his dismay, he discovered that while his team members received hikes ranging from 5% to 10%, he had only received a meagre 2% increase.

Concerned about the low hike, Aravind approached his team leader, who was already dealing with another team member's dissatisfaction over a 1% hike. Aravind questioned his team leader about the reason for the discrepancy in his hike compared to his peers. His team leader, feeling the pressure, told him bluntly to take the matter up with Senior Manager Priya Sharma, who was responsible for the salary increments.

Feeling a mix of frustration and determination, Aravind decided to confront Priya Sharma about the issue. He knew it was not going to be an easy conversation, but he needed answers. Aravind made his way to Priya Sharma's office, his mind racing with questions about why his performance was not reflected in his salary increase.

As he reached Priya Sharma's office, Aravind took a deep breath and knocked on the door. Priya Sharma invited him in and asked him what the matter was. Aravind respectfully presented his case, explaining his contributions to the team and the disparity in his hike compared to others.

Priya Sharma listened attentively; her expression thoughtful. After a moment of silence, she explained to Aravind that the hike percentages were determined based on various factors, including performance reviews, project allocations, and budget constraints. She assured him that his efforts were recognized, but due to certain constraints, the hike percentage had to be adjusted.

Though disappointed, Frustrated and disheartened by Priya Sharma's explanation, Aravind couldn't contain his emotions any longer. He felt that his hard work and dedication were not being valued appropriately. With a racing heart and a mind filled with frustration, Aravind raised his voice, expressing his discontent.

"It's based on one-sided decisions!" Aravind exclaimed; his tone filled with frustration. "Hike for certain members, I understand, mam. But I've worked day and night, and there's no certain good hikes!"

His outburst startled Priya Sharma, who tried to calm him down and explain the situation further. But Aravind was not in the mood to listen. He felt like he was being overlooked and unfairly treated despite his efforts.

"I've put in my best effort, but it seems like it's not enough," Aravind continued, his voice trembling with emotion. "I deserve better recognition for my hard work!"

Priya Sharma tried to reason with Aravind, emphasizing the constraints they were facing and the need to consider various factors in determining salary hikes. But Aravind's frustration had reached its peak.

Feeling overwhelmed and defeated, Aravind stormed out of Priya Sharma's office, his mind clouded with disappointment and anger. He couldn't shake off the feeling of injustice and inequality that lingered in his thoughts.

Back at his desk, Aravind struggled to focus on his work. The sense of disillusionment weighed heavily on him as he contemplated his future with the company. Despite his dedication and commitment, he felt unappreciated and undervalued.

As the day came to an end, Aravind left the office with a heavy heart, his mind filled with uncertainty about his career path. He knew that he needed to reflect on his options and decide what steps to take next to ensure that his efforts were truly recognized and rewarded.

Part 18

THE WEIGHT OF EMOTIONS

As Aravind reached home, he parked his bike and took a moment to compose himself. He didn't want to disturb his family with his frustrations from work. Climbing up to the eighth floor, he entered his home, greeted by a sight that only added to his irritation.

The living room was cluttered with toys scattered everywhere. Sanjay, their elder son, had his leg in the baby cycle and was engrossed in watching a TV series. Tessy was in the kitchen, cooking diligently amidst the chaos.

Aravind couldn't contain his frustration anymore. "Tessy, clean all this nonsense first!" he shouted, his voice echoing through the house. He didn't mean to be harsh, but the mess added to his already stressed state.

Feeling overwhelmed, Aravind headed straight to his room for some much-needed refreshment. He closed the door behind him, trying to shake off the tension from the day. Sitting on the bed, he took deep breaths, trying to calm his racing mind.

Meanwhile, Tessy paused her cooking and exchanged a worried glance with Sanjay. She knew Aravind was under a lot of pressure lately, but his outburst took her by surprise.

After a few minutes, Tessy entered their room, her expression softening as she saw Aravind's troubled face. "Are you okay?" she asked gently, sitting beside him on the bed.

Aravind sighed, running his hands through his hair. "I'm sorry, Tessy. It's just been a long day at work," he admitted, his voice tired.

Tessy nodded understandingly, placing a comforting hand on his shoulder. "It's alright, Aravind. We'll clean up and make everything right," she assured him, her voice soothing.

Feeling a sense of relief wash over him, Aravind leaned into Tessy's comforting embrace. Despite the chaos and stress, he knew he could always count on his family to support him through the toughest times.

Arvind sat on the edge of the bed, lost in his thoughts, his anger still simmering from the events of the day. Tessy quietly put their baby to sleep and joined with Aravind in the bedroom. She could sense that something was bothering Aravind deeply.

As Tessy sat beside him, she gently took Arvind's hand in hers and looked into his eyes with concern. "What happened today, Arvind?" she asked softly, trying to understand the source of his distress.

Arvind leaned into Tessy's embrace, feeling the weight of the day finally catching up to him. With tears welling up in his eyes, he poured out his frustrations about the unfairness he experienced at work, how he felt undervalued despite his hard work and dedication.

Tessy listened patiently, holding Arvind close and offering him the comfort he needed. As Aravind continued to speak, his voice cracking with emotion, Tessy gently stroked his back, reassuring him that she was there for him.

Feeling overwhelmed by his emotions, Arvind hugged Tessy tightly, burying his face in her shoulder as tears streamed down his cheeks. Tessy hugged him back just as tightly, whispering soothing words and gently rocking him like she would with their baby.

With Tessy's comforting presence, Arvind gradually began to calm down. He felt the weight of his anger and frustration lifting, replaced by a sense of relief and gratitude for having Tessy by his side.

Aravind hugged Tessy tightly, feeling her warmth and comfort. Tessy's embrace made Aravind's anger melt away, and he leaned in to kiss her lips. Tessy reciprocated the kiss, and Aravind felt his tension easing as their lips met. He hugged Tessy even tighter, cherishing the moment of intimacy.

Feeling the warmth of Tessy's embrace after a long time, Aravind's anger dissolved completely. He realized how much he had missed being close to her. Tessy, sensing the change in Aravind's mood, allowed him to express his affection freely.

Aravind began to kiss Tessy all over, showering her with love and affection. His anger turned into pure enjoyment as he explored every inch of her body with tenderness and passion. Tessy responded with love and openness, allowing Aravind to express his desires without hesitation.

As they shared this intimate moment, Aravind's anger faded into happiness. He realized that nothing was more important than the love and connection he shared with Tessy. In her arms, he found solace and peace, and his heart overflowed with joy.

Tessy rested her head in Aravind's hand, finding comfort in his presence. She expressed her fear to Aravind about the possibility of getting pregnant again, especially since they hadn't been using any birth control. Aravind smiled reassuringly, telling Tessy that if it happens, they will accept it wholeheartedly.

However, Tessy's mind was filled with worries about returning to work again. She was interested in restarting her career, but taking care of another baby made her hesitant, as it would make going back to work in the next three years seem impossible. She expressed her concerns to Aravind, stating that she wasn't ready for another child yet. Aravind, being the supportive husband, tried to ease her worries by saying that he understood the challenges they might face, but they would manage together as a family.

Aravind then mentioned that he was the only child in his family, and he knew the importance of having siblings. He gently hinted that Sanjay might want a sibling too, and if Tessy became pregnant again, they would be there for each other.

Despite Aravind's reassurances, Tessy still felt conflicted. On one hand, she understood the joy of having another child, but on the other hand, she worried about the added responsibilities and challenges it would bring, especially since their first baby still required a lot of attention.

As they continued their conversation, Tessy's thoughts were in turmoil. She nodded in agreement to Aravind's words, but deep down, she couldn't shake off her apprehensions about the idea of having another baby so soon.

Part 19

FROM TENSION TO TRANQUILLITY

*T*essy's monthly menstrual cycle had been delayed, raising suspicions in both her and Aravind's minds. As Aravind entered the house one evening, he carried a pregnancy test strip with him, determined to confirm their suspicions. Sanjay, seeing his dad, rushed to hug him, unaware of the tension in the air.

Aravind handed the pregnancy strip to Tessy, who took it with a mix of fear and reluctance. She entered the bathroom to conduct the test while Aravind waited anxiously outside meanwhile playing with Sanjay. Tessy's wish was not to be pregnant again so soon, as she was still adjusting to the demands of motherhood with their first child. On the other hand, Aravind secretly hoped for another baby, wanting to expand their family.

Inside the bathroom, Tessy followed the steps outlined in the manual for the strip test. With bated breath, she waited for the results. After a few moments, she looked at the strip and saw a two red line appearing. According to the instructions, one line indicated no pregnancy, while two lines confirmed pregnancy.

Tessy's heart sank as she saw two lines forming on the strip, confirming her fears. She was pregnant again. Despite her apprehensions, she had to come to terms with the reality of another child on the way.

Exiting the bathroom, Tessy hesitantly showed the strip to Aravind, who couldn't contain his excitement. Sanjay, sensing the tension, looked at his parents curiously. Aravind's face lit up with joy as he saw the two lines, but Tessy's expression remained solemn.

Tessy's mind raced with thoughts of how she would manage another pregnancy and take care of two children. Aravind, on the other hand, was thrilled at the prospect of expanding their family.

With conflicting emotions swirling between them, Tessy and Aravind faced the reality of another pregnancy, unsure of what the future held for their growing family.

Tessy and Sanjay sat in the back of the auto as its maneuverer through the crowded streets towards Sandhiya Hospital. Sanjay, full of energy, couldn't resist touching Tessy's face and playing around. Tessy, trying to focus, gently insisted that Sanjay be quiet in baby language.

As they approached the Perugudi traffic signal, the light turned red, and the auto came to a halt amidst the sea of people. It was 10:30 in the morning, and the streets were bustling with activity. Tessy felt a surge of anxiety as she observed the crowded surroundings. Her fingers started to grind, and her legs felt restless. Her heart raced with apprehension, but she tried to maintain her composure for Sanjay's sake.

Despite the overwhelming crowd and her rising anxiety, Tessy managed to soothe Sanjay and ensure they reached Sandhiya Hospital safely. As they finally arrived at their destination, Tessy heaved a sigh of relief, grateful to have navigated through the chaotic streets to reach the hospital.

Once Tessy reached the hospital and entered, the staff quickly checked her vitals and directed her to the doctor's office. As Tessy made her way through the hospital corridors, her heart pounded with anticipation. She was relieved to see familiar faces among the hospital staff, which helped ease her nerves.

When Tessy entered Doctor Shilpa's room, she was greeted with a warm smile from the doctor. Aravind, who had rushed from work to be with Tessy, also felt relieved to see Doctor Shilpa. The familiarity of Doctor Shilpa's presence reassured them both.

Evening Aravind returned home, he was taken aback to find the house in disarray, with toys strewn everywhere. Concerned, he quickly searched for Tessy, his wife, and found her sitting in the bedroom, tears streaming down her face.

Tessy looked distraught; her face flushed with emotion. Aravind was startled and asked her why she was crying, his voice tinged with frustration. Tessy, in a trembling voice, pleaded with him not to shout, explaining that she was afraid. Aravind's demeanour softened as he realized the impact of his tone on Tessy, and he slowly approached her, wrapping her in a comforting hug to calm her down.

After a while, Tessy's sobs subsided, and she wiped away her tears. She explained that she had become overwhelmed after scolding

Sanjay for scattering toys all over the room. Aravind reassured her that it was normal for children to make a mess sometimes and that she should handle Sanjay more gently.

Tessy nodded, feeling reassured by Aravind's words. She leaned into his embrace, finding solace in his presence. Aravind gently stroked her hair, promising to help clean up the mess together. As they worked side by side, the tension dissipated, replaced by a sense of unity and understanding between them.

In the dead of night, Aravind woke up feeling parched, his throat dry. He carefully tiptoed through the darkened room, not wanting to disturb Tessy who was still awake. He found his way to the kitchen, where he poured himself a glass of water under the dim glow of a low-watt bulb.

As he turned to return to bed, he noticed that Tessy was also awake, sitting up in bed with a troubled expression. Concerned, Aravind approached her and gently asked what was wrong. Tessy's voice trembled as she explained that she couldn't sleep – every time she closed her eyes, her heart pounded, and her hands shook.

Aravind felt a pang of worry for Tessy and immediately wrapped his arms around her, offering comfort. He suggested that they go to the balcony for some fresh air, hoping it would help Tessy relax. Holding her hand, Aravind led Tessy to the balcony, where they stood under the cool night sky.

The gentle breeze brushed against their faces, carrying the scent of jasmine from the nearby garden. Aravind encouraged Tessy to take deep breaths and focus on the soothing sounds of the night – the rustle of leaves, the distant chirping of crickets.

Slowly, Tessy began to calm down, her breathing steadying as she leaned against Aravind's chest. He held her close, murmuring words of reassurance and love, promising to always be there for her. Eventually, Tessy's tense muscles relaxed, and her eyelids grew heavy with sleep.

Aravind guided her back to bed, tucking her in with care before lying down beside her. As they cuddled together, the worries of the night melted away, replaced by a sense of peace and security in each other's arms.

Part 20

TESSY'S PRIDE, ARAVIND'S SUCCESS

*I*n June 20 2016, Tessy, now a mother of two sons, Sanjay and Amal, was busy cleaning the house. Her cheeks had become a little fuller from the joy of motherhood, and her days were filled with caring for her two energetic boys.

As Tessy was cleaning the bathroom, her younger son Amal, with his small and attractive face, was drawn to a memento on the top shelf of the TV showcase. The memento was a token of praise for Tessy being named the best worker of the year. The vibrant colours of the memento caught Amal's eye, and he decided he wanted it.

Amal, determined to get the memento, slowly climbed onto the TV rack. With careful steps, he made his way to the top shelf and reached for the prized object. But once he had it in his hands, he realized he didn't know how to get back down.

Unable to climb down, Amal started crying loudly, his tiny voice echoing through the house. Hearing her son's distress, Tessy rushed to the living space, her heart pounding with fear. She found Amal on the top shelf, clutching the memento tightly, tears streaming down his face.

Tessy gently scolded Amal for his reckless actions, asking him why he had climbed up there. Amal, still sobbing, held onto the memento, unable to explain his actions.

Seeing her son in distress, Tessy's stern expression softened, and she hugged him tightly. She carefully lifted Amal down from the shelf, reassuring him that everything was okay.

Tessy hugged Amal tightly as he showed her the memento he had taken from the top shelf. With tear-stained cheeks, Amal proudly presented the token of appreciation that his mother had received for her hard work.

Tessy took the memento from Amal's tiny hands and looked at it fondly. It was a reminder of her dedication and commitment to her work, a symbol of recognition for her efforts.

As Tessy smiled at the memento, memories flooded back to her—late nights at the office, long hours spent on projects, and the joy of achieving success. She remembered the pride she felt when she received the award, knowing that her hard work had been acknowledged.

Looking at the memento now, held in her son's hands, Tessy felt a surge of love and gratitude. It was a reminder of the importance of her work and the impact it had on her family.

Amal looked up at his mother with big, innocent eyes, his tears now replaced with a sense of wonder and curiosity. Tessy hugged him again, grateful for his love and understanding.

Together, mother and son shared a moment of quiet appreciation, surrounded by the warmth of their home and the love that bound them together.

Aravind stood proudly on stage as Naveen Kishore, the Managing Director of Coretronix Techno Solutions, presented him with an award for his outstanding achievement in the UK-based project. The applause filled the room, and Aravind felt a swell of pride in his chest.

In his speech, Mr. Naveen Kishore praised Aravind's dedication and hard work, emphasizing that the company recognized and appreciated its employees' efforts. Aravind's colleagues cheered and clapped, happy to see him receive the recognition he deserved.

However, not everyone shared in the celebration. Priya Sharma, now the delivery head at the company, sat in the audience, her expression clouded with irritation. Three years ago, Aravind had clashed with Priya, and the memory still lingered, souring her mood despite the festive atmosphere.

Aravind, though aware of Priya's displeasure, remained focused on the positive moment. He was proud of his achievements and grateful for the recognition. Moreover, he had recently been promoted to a team leader position in a new project, adding to his sense of accomplishment.

As the ceremony concluded, Aravind received congratulations from his colleagues and exchanged smiles with his friends. Despite the lingering tension with Priya, Aravind was determined to continue excelling in his work and proving his worth to the company.

Aravind returned home with a wide smile on his face, his heart brimming with happiness from the day's events. Sanjay was diligently working on his homework at the dining table, his textbooks spread out before him. Aravind set down his briefcase and greeted his son with a warm pat on the back, admiring his dedication to his studies.

Tessy, noticing Aravind's cheerful demeanour, welcomed him with a curious smile. "What's the happy news?" she asked, her eyes twinkling with anticipation.

Aravind beamed proudly and lifted both Sanjay and Amal into his arms. "Today, my Managing Director said proudly to everyone," he announced, his voice filled with excitement.

Sanjay and Amal exchanged puzzled glances, not quite understanding what their father meant, but they eagerly accepted the cakes and chocolates he offered them.

Aravind leaned in and planted a kiss on each of his children's foreheads. "It means Daddy did something really good at work," he explained, ruffling their hair affectionately.

Tessy's face lit up with pride as she realized the significance of Aravind's achievement. "That's wonderful news!" she exclaimed, wrapping her arms around her family.

Together, they shared a joyful moment, basking in the happiness of Aravind's success. And as Sanjay continued with his homework and Amal giggled in his father's arms, the warmth of their love filled the room.

Part 21

THROUGH THICK AND THIN

As Sanjay and Amal peacefully slept in their beds, Aravind gently caressed Tessy's cheeks and forehead. Tessy couldn't help but smile at his touch, feeling the warmth of his love. Aravind, admiring his wife, teasingly remarked, "Even though you've gained a little weight, you look as beautiful as ever."

Tessy, playfully indignant, responded, "You're always able to exercise because I take care of all the family responsibilities."

Aravind chuckled, "But taking care of the family is also a lot of work. Just look at the competition in the office nowadays."

Tessy felt a pang of anxiety at the mention of work. "I want to go back to work too," she admitted, feeling the weight of her long absence from the workforce.

Aravind teased her gently, "At your age, with such a long gap in your job, how will you manage to get a job?"

Tessy's tension increased, and she pleaded with Aravind to stop. "Please, Aravind, let's not fight."

Aravind sensed Tessy's unease and reached out to comfort her. "I'm in a romantic mood tonight. Let's not argue," he said, touching her forehead affectionately.

Feeling somewhat reassured, Aravind hugged Tessy tightly. As they embraced, Tessy couldn't shake off her concerns completely. "Do you have protection?" she asked Aravind, her voice tinged with worry.

Aravind nodded with a smile. "Yes," he reassured her, holding her close.

With that, they put aside their worries for the moment, focusing instead on the love and connection they shared. As they drifted off to sleep, wrapped in each other's arms, they knew they could face whatever challenges lay ahead as long as they were together.

Part 22

UNSEEN STRUGGLES

As Aravind left for work and Sanjay headed to school, Amal is playing in living area with his toys, Tessy began her daily chores, cleaning the vessels in their eighth-floor apartment. While washing the dishes, Tessy glanced out of the window and saw the bustling parking lot below, filled with young women rushing off to work. Suddenly, Tessy felt her heart race, and her vision began to blur. She tried to turn away, but her body felt frozen in place.

Feeling hopeless and terrified, Tessy slowly made her way to the living area where Amal was playing. Her hands trembled, and she broke out in a cold sweat. Fear gripped her as she thought she might be having a heart attack. Unable to move, Tessy reached for her phone and dialled the security guard's number, her voice shaking as she described her symptoms.

In a panic, Tessy called Aravind, her husband, and explained her situation. Aravind, alarmed by Tessy's distress, immediately turned back home to check on her. Meanwhile, the security guard arrived and called for an emergency ambulance.

As Tessy was rushed to WellCare 24-hour Mult speciality Hospital, her mind raced with fear. What if it was a heart attack?

What would happen to her children? Aravind prayed fervently as he raced to the hospital, his heart heavy with worry.

At the hospital, doctors quickly attended to Tessy, running tests to determine the cause of her symptoms. Tessy was terrified, but she found solace in the presence of the medical staff. Aravind arrived just in time to see Tessy being taken for further examination.

Hours passed, and after a thorough evaluation, the doctors informed Aravind that Tessy was not experiencing a heart attack but rather a severe panic attack brought on by stress and anxiety. Relieved but still shaken, Aravind thought that it wasn't something more serious.

The doctors recommended rest and relaxation for Tessy, along with counselling to manage her stress and anxiety. Aravind promised to support Tessy every step of the way, and together they faced the challenge of overcoming Tessy's panic attacks.

As they left the hospital, Tessy held Aravind's hand tightly, grateful for his unwavering support. Though shaken by the experience, Tessy knew that with Aravind by her side, she could face anything that came her way.

Aravind and Tessy sat nervously in the office of Doctor K. Udayamohan, the famous psychiatrist at WellCare Hospital. Doctor Udayamohan, a calm and composed figure with short hair and glasses, listened attentively as Tessy explained her physical symptoms and feelings of fear and hopelessness. Aravind held Tessy's hand tightly, his concern evident on his face.

Tessy described how her hands always seemed to be in pain and how she constantly felt a burning sensation. She expressed her fear and hopelessness, which seemed to overshadow her daily life.

After a thorough examination, Doctor Udayamohan diagnosed Tessy with postpartum depression and social anxiety disorder. He explained to Aravind that these were serious conditions that required attention.

Aravind, however, seemed hesitant to accept the severity of the situation. He suggested that Tessy's symptoms might be due to laziness. But Doctor Udayamohan quickly corrected him, explaining that mental illness is not a matter of laziness but rather a complex interaction between the brain and external factors.

The psychiatrist recommended medication to help alleviate Tessy's symptoms, but he also stressed the importance of therapy. He suggested that Tessy see a psychologist, Miss Divya Priya, who could provide guidance and support.

Aravind listened to the doctor's advice, though he still seemed sceptical. However, he understood that Tessy needed help, and he was willing to support her in any way he could.

Tessy had been taking her medications for two weeks, and although she felt somewhat better, her nervousness persisted. One evening, as Aravind was teaching Sanjay about mathematics, Tessy entered the living area and sat down on the sofa beside them.

"Tessy, what's on your mind?" Aravind asked, noticing her sombre expression.

Tessy hesitated for a moment before speaking up. "The medications are helping, but I still don't feel fully recovered. I think I need to see Miss Divya Priya, the psychologist."

Aravind's initial reaction was one of irritation. "Why do you keep wanting to go to the hospital? I can't keep taking leave from work every time you need to visit a doctor," he said, his frustration evident.

Tessy understood Aravind's concerns, but she knew she needed more than just medication to overcome her anxiety. "I know it's counselling, but I think it will help me," she said softly.

Aravind sighed, "Alright, we'll go,"

Part 23

PSYCHOLOGIST (NOT PSYCHIATRIST)

Aravind and Tessy sat in front of Miss Divya Priya, surrounded by shelves of books on human behaviour and psychology. Divya Priya welcomed them with a warm smile, her youthful appearance putting Tessy at ease.

"Let's start by talking about yourself and the problems you've been facing," Divya Priya said, initiating the session.

Tessy felt a sense of hope as she began to open up to the psychologist. She talked about her background, her studies, and her struggles with managing two children for the past five years. Tessy expressed her feelings of exhaustion and hopelessness, particularly regarding her responsibilities at home and her husband's attitude towards her work.

Aravind, sitting quietly, felt a twinge of irritation as Tessy repeated familiar complaints. Divya Priya noticed his demeanour and gently asked him to step outside for a moment so she could speak with Tessy privately.

Outside the cabin, Aravind waited, feeling a mix of frustration and concern. He wondered if this counselling session would really help Tessy.

Meanwhile, inside the cabin, Tessy continued to pour her heart out to Divya Priya. She spoke about how she used to feel happy and confident while working, but now she often felt overwhelmed and lost.

Divya Priya listened intently, observing Tessy's body language and tone as she spoke. After an hour of discussion, Divya Priya reached a conclusion and asked Aravind to rejoin them.

Aravind entered the room, his expression reflecting his inner turmoil. Divya Priya addressed him directly, "Aravind, Tessy has been facing significant challenges, and it's important for both of you to understand her struggles."

Divya Priya explained Tessy's feelings of stress and hopelessness, emphasizing the importance of empathy and support from her family, especially Aravind.

Aravind listened attentively as Divya Priya suggested ways for him to provide better support for Tessy and encouraged open communication between them.

Divya Priya, the psychologist, looked at Aravind with a calm yet firm gaze. "Now I understand your wife's concerns," she said. "These feelings are common among women living in cities nowadays."

Tessy's face showed a mix of relief and apprehension as Divya Priya continued. "Actually, she is alright, but she needs 5 to 6 counselling sessions," the psychologist explained. She turned to Aravind and emphasized, "She will be much better when she starts working again."

Aravind hesitated, citing the difficulty of finding someone to take care of the children if Tessy went back to work. Divya Priya nodded understandingly. "That's her problem," she said gently. "For the past five years, she has been shouldering the family duties alone, and she's exhausted. Please allow her to go back to work."

Divya Priya, the psychologist, looked at Aravind with a gentle yet firm expression. "Aravind, I understand that you have your commitments, but right now, Tessy needs your support more than ever," she began. Aravind nodded, listening intently as Divya Priya continued. "I suggest that you take care of the children for the next six months and consider taking a leave from your job. This will give Tessy the opportunity to go back to work and focus on her own well-being."

Aravind listened but remained unconvinced. "But, Mam, I am a team leader and soon to be promoted to manager in my office. I earn nearly one lakh in salary. If Tessy goes to work, how much could she possibly earn?" he questioned.

Divya Priya sighed, realizing the depth of Aravind's misunderstanding. "It's not just about the money," she explained patiently. "Tessy needs the independence, the fulfilment, and the sense of purpose that comes with working. It's essential for her well-being."

Aravind remained silent, mulling over Divya Priya's words. Tessy, feeling frustrated with her husband's lack of understanding, shifted uncomfortably in her seat.

Divya Priya then suggested that Aravind take a week off from his commitments and take Tessy to a natural place for some relaxation. Aravind immediately dismissed the idea, saying it was impossible with his workload.

The psychologist's tone became more serious. "You're not understanding the severity of the problem," she said firmly. "If you continue like this, Tessy's mental health could deteriorate further."

Tessy felt a surge of anger at her husband's dismissive attitude. She had been silently carrying the burden of their family responsibilities for too long, and now she needed his support more than ever.

After the session, Aravind reflected on Divya Priya's words. He realized that he needed to prioritize Tessy's well-being over his work commitments. Tessy, though still upset, felt grateful that someone was finally listening to her. She hoped that her husband would soon understand her needs and support her decision to go back to work.

Part 24

A BEACON OF HOPE

Tessy's tired face was marked by dark circles under her eyes, and her weak hair, along with her poorly dressed appearance, hinted at her exhaustion. Tessy stood by the balcony, her mind clouded with thoughts and her heart heavy with burden. The sound of Amal crying echoed in the background, adding to her distress. Tessy felt overwhelmed, her emotions threatening to consume her.

In a moment of frustration, Tessy hurried to the bedroom and picked up Amal to soothe him. After settling him down, she returned to the balcony, her mind still racing with disturbing thoughts. She glanced down at the ground below, contemplating the idea of ending her suffering by jumping.

But amidst the turmoil, Tessy found a spark of resilience within herself. She fought against the dark thoughts, determined not to succumb to them. With a deep breath, she pushed herself away from the edge and resolved to seek help.

Tessy made her way to Miss Divya Priya, her psychologist, seeking solace and guidance. As she poured out her troubles,

Divya Priya listened attentively, her calm demeanour offering a sense of comfort.

Divya Priya gently reminded Tessy that while medications may provide temporary relief, they couldn't address the root of her problems. She emphasized the importance of therapy in uncovering and addressing the underlying issues causing Tessy's distress.

As Tessy sat across from psychologist Divya Priya, she felt a mix of emotions stirring within her. Divya Priya's gentle yet probing questions touched upon sensitive topics, bringing to light Tessy's inner struggles.

"Why do you go to your parent's home for making yourself happy?" Divya Priya asked, her tone soft yet probing.

Tessy hesitated for a moment, her mind flickering back to memories of her past. She had been in a love marriage against her parents' wishes, a decision that had strained their relationship.

With a heavy heart, Tessy replied, "My parents never came for my death also."

Her words hung in the air, weighted with the pain of unresolved conflicts and shattered expectations. Tessy had longed for her parents' acceptance and support, but instead, she had faced rejection and disapproval.

Divya Priya listened attentively; her eyes filled with empathy as she recognized the deep-seated wounds Tessy carried within her. She understood that Tessy's struggles went beyond the surface, rooted in years of familial discord and emotional turmoil.

As their session progressed, Divya Priya gently guided Tessy towards exploring her own sources of strength and resilience. She encouraged Tessy to focus on building a support system outside of her family, one that would nurture and uplift her in times of need.

With each session, Tessy began to unravel the layers of her pain and find the courage to confront her past. Divya Priya provided a safe space for Tessy to heal, offering guidance and support as she navigated the complexities of her emotions.

Though the road ahead was filled with challenges, Tessy felt a glimmer of hope within her heart. With Divya Priya's help, she knew she could begin to heal from the wounds of her past and forge a path towards a brighter, more fulfilling future.

Tessy realized that overcoming her problems required support from her husband, so she called Aravind, who was in his office leading his team. Aravind was in a conference room, instructing his team with his matured face and commanding voice. The newly joined team members listened carefully as Aravind outlined the next week's tasks.

Part 25

BEYOND THE EDGE

"Team, we have the final product delivery to the client next week. We need to put in extra hours to complete the project. I'm with you every step of the way," Aravind said confidently.

As Aravind's phone rang, he excused himself from the conference to take the call from Tessy. He assured her that he would call her back later without asking anything further.

Tessy made herself bold, knowing that she would speak with him in the evening. She understood the importance of discussing her concerns with Aravind and hoped that he would be supportive and understanding.

Aravind returned home to find the house neat and clean, a sight that brought a smile to his face. Tessy looked well, much better than she had in a long time. Aravind greeted her with a smile and asked, "Are you okay?"

Tessy smiled back and replied, "I'm almost okay, but I need your help."

Aravind nodded and went to freshen up. Meanwhile, Sanjay was studying diligently in the study room. Aravind peeked into the room, seeing his son focused on his studies. He couldn't help but feel proud.

"My son!" Aravind exclaimed; his voice filled with pride as he saw Sanjay's dedication to his studies. Sanjay smiled in response, appreciating the encouragement from his father.

It was 10 o'clock at night, and the children had finally fallen asleep. Tessy took Aravind by the hand and led him to the balcony. She put on a smile, trying to hide her inner turmoil, and looked at Aravind.

"Please listen to me, Aravind," Tessy said softly, her voice trembling slightly.

Aravind nodded, his expression serious, and encouraged her to continue.

Tessy took a deep breath and confessed, "I understand that I have a problem. I have severe anxiety disorder and depression, but I need to overcome this. I need your help."

Aravind listened intently as Tessy poured her heart out. She explained how she felt overwhelmed by racing thoughts, how her hands and chest would vibrate with anxiety. She pleaded with Aravind to spend just one week with her, to help her through this difficult time.

But Aravind hesitated. In his mind, he couldn't comprehend the severity of Tessy's condition. To him, it seemed like something she could easily overcome.

Tessy continued, expressing her loneliness and the monotony of her routine over the past six years. She knew that many women faced similar challenges, but not all of them experienced such intense mental health struggles. She begged Aravind for his support, emphasizing that her well-being was more important than anything else.

However, Aravind was reluctant. He explained that he couldn't take time off work, especially with an important project deadline approaching. He mentioned the possibility of an onsite opportunity after the completion of the project, which he couldn't risk by taking leave.

Tessy persisted, pleading with Aravind to reconsider, even if it was just for Three Days. But Aravind remained firm in his decision, stating that it was simply not possible for him to take time off.

Tessy's face fell, her eyes turning red with tears. She felt crushed by Aravind's refusal, the weight of her struggles heavier than ever. Silently, Aravind got up and left for the room, leaving Tessy alone on the balcony with her thoughts.

Feeling defeated and helpless, Tessy wiped away her tears and stared out into the night, longing for the support and understanding she so desperately needed.

As Tessy stood alone on the balcony, her mind raced with thoughts of despair. The idea of jumping from the eighth floor crossed her mind, but she pushed it away, knowing it wasn't a solution. She couldn't sleep; her racing thoughts kept her awake until 2:00 a.m. Her chest tightened, and she felt increasingly hopeless.

Desperate for relief, Tessy went to the kitchen to drink water. She called out to Aravind, but he was fast asleep and didn't respond. Feeling more isolated than ever, Tessy returned to the balcony and sat on the bean bag, attempting to find some semblance of peace.

But sleep evaded her. Every tick of the clock felt like an eternity, and the sound of the clock's pendulum only added to her irritation. Tessy's anxiety continued to rise, and she waited anxiously for the sun to rise, longing for the darkness to dissipate.

Part 26

ALONE IN THE DARK

By 6:00 a.m., Tessy was exhausted. She went back to the bedroom just as Aravind woke up and headed to freshen up. Tessy waited in the living area, her eyes swollen and her face worn out. Her hair was dishevelled, a reflection of her inner turmoil.

Feeling overwhelmed, Tessy checked her heart rate while closing her eyes, but it only made her anxiety worse. She took some prescribed medication to calm herself, but the anxiety persisted.

Aravind emerged from the bedroom dressed in his formal office attire, ready to leave for work. Tessy mustered the courage to ask him for just one day of his time. She pleaded with him, explaining that she was feeling completely distraught and needed his support.

Aravind's reaction was unexpected. Instead of understanding, he became irritated and demanded to know the exact problem. Tessy begged him once again for just one day, but Aravind's frustration grew.

"You and your children eat peacefully because of me," Aravind snapped. "Without going to work, how can we live happily?"

Tessy felt her heart sink at his words. She knew Aravind worked hard to provide for their family, but she also needed his emotional support. Despite her pleas, Aravind remained resolute and left for work, leaving Tessy standing silently near the television, feeling more alone than ever.

Tessy's mind was in turmoil as she made a difficult decision. Despite her love for Aravind, she couldn't bear the thought of continuing to live in anxiety and loneliness. She had sacrificed so much for him, but his unwillingness to spend even a day with her during her time of need was the final straw.

With a heavy heart, Tessy decided to leave. She packed her belongings, including her hard-earned jewellery and savings, and make woke Sanjay and Amal, preparing them for departure. As they slept peacefully, unaware of the turmoil unfolding, Tessy left the house, determined to start anew.

When Aravind returned home that evening, he was shocked to find Tessy and the children gone. Panic set in as he called her phone, only to find it switched off. Realizing Tessy's connection to her friend Jasy Sebastian, he rushed to her home.

At Jasy's door, Aravind's heart pounded with anxiety. He called out for Tessy, pleading with her to come back home. Tessy opened the door, her eyes filled with determination. She told Aravind she wasn't interested in living with him anymore.

Aravind was stunned, tears welling in his eyes as he asked why she was doing this. Tessy's anger boiled over as she shouted that she couldn't bear to see his face anymore. She reminded him of her plea for just one day of his time, a plea he had callously ignored.

Feeling hopeless and overwhelmed, Tessy cried out that if he kept asking, she would rather die with her children. With those words, she closed the door, shutting Aravind out.

Outside, Aravind was overcome with grief and remorse. He realized the depth of Tessy's pain and the consequences of his actions. As he walked alone on the road, he knew he had lost his family, and the weight of his mistakes weighed heavily on his shoulders.

Part 27

THE DIVORCE BATTLE

JULY 10TH 2019

As Tessy and Ramya waited outside the Guindy Family Court, tension hung in the air. The court was always bustling with various family issues, especially divorce cases. Ramya, Tessy's advocate, wore the traditional black gown, signifying her role as an advocate. She was accompanied by two practitioners, her assistants.

At a local tea shop nearby, the owner greeted them and took their order. Ramya ordered three teas and one coffee. Tessy's agitation was palpable, and she questioned Ramya about the sudden court summons. Ramya explained that it was Aravind, Tessy's husband, who had petitioned the court. The divorce proceedings had been prolonged for three years because Aravind was contesting the divorce, making the process longer than usual.

Ramya's assistant informed her that their case would start in half an hour, prompting Ramya to drink her tea quickly and hurry back to the court. Tessy offered to pay for the tea before they left for the court.

The Divorce Battle

Tessy's heart sank as she entered the court premises, feeling alone amidst the sea of families supporting their loved ones through divorce proceedings. The old, red-painted building stood like a fortress; its corners adorned with round-shaped ball structures reminiscent of the British colonial era.

As Tessy stepped into the court entrance, she observed the ongoing proceedings. A family court Respected judge presided over a case, investigating two individuals while Aravind stood opposite them with a calm demeanour. Tessy couldn't help but feel a pang of unease, knowing that her own divorce case would soon be underway.

Tessy felt a sense of isolation as she approached the imposing red-brick building housing the family court. The grandeur of the colonial-era architecture only added to her unease. Inside, the atmosphere was tense as families awaited their turn before the judge.

In the courtroom, Tessy observed the judge attentively questioning two individuals while Aravind stood opposite them. His composed demeanour contrasted sharply with Tessy's own anxiety. She couldn't shake the feeling of being alone in this daunting legal process.

After some time, Tessy's case was called, and she went with her advocate Ramya, while Aravind went with his Advocate Gulam Nabi Azad. Tessy and Aravind stood opposite each other, with their respective advocates by their sides. Respected Judge Mr. G. Govindraju (GG), a 55-year aged man, sat in his wooden chair with a sense of authority, poised to dispense justice. he wore a black gown and had a straightforward demeanour.

The judge questioned Aravind's Advocate about the petition, who explained that Aravind needed to take his children to see their grandmother, who was bedridden due to a brain stroke. Tessy couldn't control her emotions and shouted that she wouldn't allow her children to go with him. The judge reprimanded Tessy's outburst, and Tessy's advocate asked her to remain silent.

The judge then asked Ramya for her argument. Ramya replied that they couldn't allow Aravind to take the children, emphasizing Tessy's concerns for their safety. Tessy then spoke up, expressing her lack of trust in Aravind's ability to care for their children, which was the reason for her filing for divorce.

After hearing both sides, the judge rendered her judgment. Despite Aravind's past actions, the judge recognized the importance of his request to see his children and granted him permission to take them for three days. The judge also offered Tessy the option to accompany her children if she wished, with Aravind covering all expenses. Aravind agreed, but Tessy declined, allowing her children to go with him.

The morning session of the court ended with the judge's decision, leaving both Tessy and Aravind with mixed emotions about the outcome.

Part 28

THE MOTORCYCLE RIDE

Sanjay and Amal were getting ready for school in a hurry. Tessy, feeling exhausted from the events of the previous day, hadn't slept well and her eyes were red from crying all night. She hadn't cooked anything and was lost in her thoughts.

Suddenly, Tessy's phone rang, and the caller ID showed the name of the watchman. She answered the call, and the watchman informed her that someone named Aravind was waiting to see her. Tessy instructed the watchman to have him wait in the lounge.

As Sanjay finished getting ready and Amal buttoned his shirt, he asked his mom what they were having for breakfast. Tessy hesitated for a moment, then reluctantly revealed that their father, Aravind, had taken them to their grandparents' home for four days. Amal's face lit up with excitement upon hearing the news, but then he quickly quieted down after seeing his mother's expression.

Sanjay, on the other hand, expressed his reluctance to go with Aravind. He told his mom that he didn't want to go, but Tessy insisted, saying, "I am your mother, and I am telling you to go with your father. It's my wish."

As Tessy realized her children hadn't eaten anything yet, she sprang into action. Urgently, she moved to the kitchen and started preparing breakfast. She made egg omelette with bread, ensuring it was quick yet nutritious. Meanwhile, Amal was happily giving different expressions to his brother, Sanjay, and dancing around the room. He grabbed his uniform and decided to wear a t-shirt and jeans with his favourite small cooler on his face.

At the entrance, Amal eagerly put on his light shoes that emitted colourful lights while walking. Sanjay watched all of this quietly. Tessy finished preparing breakfast and searched for milk in the refrigerator, pouring it into a glass. Carrying the food into the living room, she couldn't help but smile at Amal's enthusiasm despite her own pain from missing their father.

The children started eating, and Amal ate quickly. Tessy packed their dresses, and Amal proudly declared that he had prepared his bag himself. Tessy checked Amal's bag and found that everything was packed correctly.

As Tessy and her children entered the lift, she reminded them not to engage in any unnecessary activities. Amal was lost in his own imagination during the ride down. When they reached the ground floor, Tessy led her children to the visitors' waiting lounge in the apartment complex, located near the cricket net practice area.

Aravind was sitting there, wearing a t-shirt and jeans with casual shoes, looking somewhat younger and relaxed. He was happily swiping through his social media feed on his phone. Tessy silently approached him, her heart pounding with a mix of emotions.

Aravind looked up from his phone as Tessy neared. Their eyes met, and for a moment, the room seemed to fade away, leaving just the two of them. Tessy's presence brought a rush of memories flooding back for Aravind. He felt a pang of guilt mixed with longing and regret.

Tessy stood before him; her expression unreadable. She hesitated for a moment before speaking softly, "Aravind, can we talk?" Her voice trembled slightly, betraying the turmoil within her.

Aravind stood silently, listening to Tessy as she spoke. Meanwhile, Amal gave a happy welcome signal with his hand. Tessy continued, addressing Aravind, "Sanjay will listen to whatever you say, but Amal is different. He's fond of chocolates and snacks and hesitates to eat anything else, even if it's necessary. He gets sick easily, so I've put some necessary medicines in this bag."

Tessy handed Aravind a black-coloured medium-sized handy pouch, showing him the medications inside for fever and cough. She then showed him two travel bags, medium-sized Sky bags. "The blue one belongs to Amal," she said, "and he's packed his clothes correctly. The black one is Sanjay's."

Tessy insisted that the children bathe on their own and dress properly. Aravind agreed silently to everything Tessy said.

As they prepared to leave, Tessy instructed Aravind not to let the children sit near the AC in the car and to make sure they wear their seat belts in the backseat. However, Aravind confessed that he had come on his motorcycle. Tessy grew tense, worried about how the children would manage such a long journey on the bike.

Amal, overhearing the conversation, shouted happily about his dad fulfilling his dream of traveling on a bike. Tessy remained silent, her worries increasing about the safety of her children on the bike.

After understanding Tessy's worries about traveling on the bike, Aravind called out to her in a soft voice. Tessy, hearing the gentleness in Aravind's tone, felt a flood of memories rushing back. Aravind assured her, "It's only 150 kilometres. We'll stop every thirty minutes to rest. Don't worry."

Aravind continued, "If the children are uncomfortable, I'll arrange for a cab instead of the bike. I'll take care of them, Tessy. You don't need to worry."

Meanwhile, Amal kept insisting that he wanted to ride on the bike, and Tessy eventually allowed him to go with Aravind. Amal, thrilled to be fulfilling his dream of riding on a bike with his dad, enjoyed every moment of the journey.

With Aravind's reassurance and trust, they embarked on the journey.

Aravind drove the bike cautiously, keeping Tessy and the children's safety in mind. Along the way, they stopped every half hour as promised, giving the children a chance to stretch and rest.

Tessy watched as her children climbed onto their daddy's motorcycle in the parking area. Aravind sat on the bike, putting on his helmet, while Amal exclaimed how much he loved the sound of the bike's engine. With Aravind's help, Amal got onto the front seat, eagerly imitating the motion of riding the bike.

Sanjay stood silently nearby, showing no interest in going. Tessy encouraged him to join, and Aravind lovingly persuaded him, "Come, Sanjay, sit on the bike with me." With a mix of reluctance and resignation, Sanjay finally agreed. Aravind started the engine of his favourite Royal Enfield bike, a sound that filled Tessy's heart with memories. She watched Aravind silently, feeling a rush of emotions.

Aravind handed small helmets to both children, Tessy feeling relieved by his care for them. Aravind bid them goodbye, and Amal happily waved while Sanjay's face showed sadness as he said his goodbye.

As the bike rode off, Tessy watched them disappear into the distance, feeling a mix of emotions—worry for her children's safety, gratitude for Aravind's care, and a sense of emptiness as she stood alone in the parking area.

Part 29

A MOUNTAIN HOMECOMING

Aravind embarked on his journey towards Vellore, navigating through the bustling Chennai traffic. He made sure to stop every thirty minutes, ensuring the safety and comfort of his children. As they reached Sriperumbudur, Amal suddenly exclaimed that he needed to pee. Aravind quickly searched for a restroom along the highway and found one at the tollgate. However, Amal insisted he didn't know how to clean himself afterward, so Aravind had to assist him for the first time. As he helped his son, Aravind couldn't help but think of Tessy and how she would have handled the situation.

Once back on the road, they continued their journey, passing through Arcot, known for its delicious star biryani. Aravind decided to treat his children to a meal, buying biryani for them. Amal eagerly dug into his food, but Sanjay refused to eat. Seeing his brother's reluctance, Amal reassured Aravind, "Don't worry, Daddy. If Sanjay doesn't want to eat, I'll eat for him!" With determination, Amal grabbed a leg piece and took a hearty bite, showing his support for his brother.

Aravind smiled at his sons' bond and continued their journey towards Vellore, grateful for their resilience and love for each other.

Sanjay held onto the water can, taking sips as his father rode the bike. As they entered Vellore, Aravind pointed out the city's mountainous landscape, explaining that they were surrounded by hills. Amal, feeling tired, asked how much longer they had to travel. Aravind reassured him that it would be another hour.

Amal expressed his desire to rest, but Aravind promised him a treat from a famous ice cream parlour in Vellore. They made their way to Maharani Ice Creams, where Aravind joined the long queue to order. Sanjay was excited to see the variety of ice creams offered. When asked if he wanted some, Sanjay declined.

Aravind ordered three ice creams and almond milk juices, but Sanjay refused to eat. Aravind didn't force him and instead gave the remaining treats to some beggars nearby. Amal happily savoured his ice cream, and though Aravind didn't eat, he was content seeing his son enjoy the treat. They continued their journey, with Amal feeling rejuvenated after his ice cream break.

As the clock struck 3:00 PM, Aravind started up his motorcycle after their ice cream break. They set off towards Arni Road, heading for the Amirthi Forest. The road led them into a zone filled with lush greenery, surrounded by mountains adorned with bamboo, teakwood, and sandalwood trees. This area was known as the Eastern Ghats, located in the Tiruvannamalai district of Tamil Nadu.

Sanjay couldn't contain his excitement at the sight of the picturesque nature around them, while Amal felt a bit fearful of the dense forest. Aravind confidently guided his bike through the winding roads as they entered the forest check post.

At the check post, they encountered a formidable forest officer, towering in height and built like a mountain. He sternly asked Aravind where they were headed, expressing concern about the dense forest. Aravind calmly explained that they were heading to the mountain town of Jamunamaruthar, nestled within these very mountains.

The forest officer, intrigued by Aravind's claim, inquired if he was truly from that dense forest town. Aravind confidently produced his ID proof, confirming his connection to the village. Impressed by Aravind's authenticity, the forest officer removed the check post and allowed them to proceed on their journey.

Aravind confidently maneuverer his bike through the lush greenery, with trees lining both sides of the road. As they rode, they came across a small river flowing gracefully from the mountains, its clear waters reflecting the sunlight. Ahead of them stood great mountains, their peaks disappearing into the clouds.

Sanjay gazed in wonder at the majestic mountains, his eyes sparkling with joy at the sight. He was fascinated by the natural beauty surrounding them. Amal, on the other hand, felt a bit more apprehensive, intimidated by the vastness of the mountains.

Noticing Amal's unease, Aravind reassured his children, "Don't worry, I'm right here with you. These mountains may seem big, but we're safe together." His words brought a sense of comfort to Amal, who gradually began to relax as they continued their journey through the breathtaking landscape.

Aravind began to ascend the mountain on his bike, navigating the winding roads that led to Jamunamaruthar, a significant town nestled in the Eastern Ghats of the Jawadhu Hills in Tamil Nadu. These hills were home to numerous villages scattered across their expanse, spanning the districts of Tiruvannamalai, Vellore, and Tirupattur.

As they rode, the roads hugged the edges of the hills, offering breathtaking views of the landscape below. The lush greenery and the gentle breeze made it feel like they were in paradise. Aravind confidently maneuverer his bike along the winding roads, while Amal closed his eyes tightly, feeling a bit scared of the heights. Sanjay, however, found solace in holding onto his father's shoulder, his trust in Aravind giving him courage.

Feeling Sanjay's grip on his shoulder, Aravind smiled softly, finding comfort in his son's trust. He continued to navigate the mountain roads, the scenic beauty of the hills soothing his soul as they journeyed deeper into the heart of the Jawadhu Hills.

Sanjay admired the scenery as they rode along the river, feeling the gentle breeze and watching the water flow beside them. Aravind kept a steady pace on the bike, navigating the curves of the road with ease. He encouraged Amal to open his eyes and take in the beauty around them, but the young boy, still feeling fearful, hesitated.

Suddenly, Sanjay's excitement erupted as he spotted an elephant crossing in the distance among the trees. He eagerly pointed it out to Amal, who slowly opened his eyes to see. As they continued riding, the buildings below began to look smaller, indicating they were gaining altitude.

Aravind navigated through the curves and hairpin bends of the mountain roads, his sons experiencing a mix of excitement and trepidation. They passed by roadworks, where workers were busy cleaning and rebuilding the road due to landslides caused by the rainy season.

In the midst of their journey, they encountered several small waterfalls, their soothing sounds mixing with the chirping of birds and the gentle breeze. Sanjay's joy was evident as he leaned against his father's shoulder, finding comfort in the familiar presence.

Aravind couldn't help but smile at his son's happiness as they continued their journey towards Jamunamaruthar, with a signboard indicating they were just 12 kilometres away.

As Aravind entered Jamunamaruthar in the Jawathu Hills, he noticed a stark difference in the animals compared to those in the cities. The cows, though thin to look at, appeared very healthy and fertile. They roamed freely on the hills, along with goats and chickens, each species adapted to the hilly terrain.

In this mountainous region, it was normal for every animal to be robust and capable of running fast. Aravind observed the cows running gracefully on the hillsides, while the goats and chickens also seemed agile and energetic.

Upon entering Jamunamaruthar, Aravind passed by the forest office and continued into the market area. It was already 5:30

PM, and people were busy buying fresh produce like carrots and beetroots with their leaves still attached. Amal, excited by the bustling market, eagerly opened his eyes to take in the sights and sounds of the hill town.

As Aravind crossed the market, he reached the end where several sub-streets branched off. He continued down the second street named Beeman Falls Street, which led to the magnificent Beeman Falls known for its natural beauty. Aravind chose this route as it was closest to the falls.

While passing by, Aravind pointed out Jawadhu Hills Primary School to his children. He shared with them that he had studied there, and even their grandfather had worked as a headmaster. Sanjay and Amal looked at the school with interest, especially Sanjay who seemed to like it a lot. The school overlooked the mountains and the sound of the nearby waterfall softly echoed in the background. Children were playing joyfully outside, and Amal expressed his desire to join them, but also mentioned his dedication to studying.

Aravind reminisced about his strict grandfather, who was both feared at home and in school. Eventually, they reached home, an oldest architecture with modest 2BHK house with terracotta roofing in a striking red colour. Wooden pillars flanked the entrance door, welcoming them back to their mountain abode. Aravind opened the gate, rode the bike inside, and slowly entered the house with his children.

Part 30

LOVE ACROSS GENERATIONS

Ravivaruman opened the door and his face lit up with happiness upon seeing Aravind, As Aravind and his children entered the house, they were greeted by a man with a bald head and round spectacles – Aravind's father, Ravivaruman. Ravivaruman was a retired headmaster and a native of Jamunamaruthur. He was the first person in his village to earn a degree and had dedicated his life to working in his hometown.

He smiled warmly at his son but immediately expressed concern about Aravind's mode of transport. He asked why Aravind had come by bike, voicing his worries about the dangers of riding.

Aravind, feeling a mix of emotions, bowed his head and remained silent. This was not the first time he had encountered his father's strictness and concern. In his younger years, Aravind had always been afraid of his father, who had a stern demeanour and emphasized the importance of doing good and avoiding trouble. Aravind had always been fonder of his mother's love and care.

However, to Aravind's surprise, Ravivaruman stepped forward and hugged his grandchildren, Sanjay and Amal, with a handful of love. This act of affection was unexpected for Aravind, who had rarely seen his father express such warmth before. Ravivaruman held the children close, his face softening with love.

Despite his initial hesitation, Aravind felt a sense of relief seeing his father's affectionate side. He followed Ravivaruman into the house, watching as his father led the children inside. At 62 years old, Ravivaruman still had the strength and love to hold his grandchildren close. As Aravind entered the house, he wondered where his mother was resting and quietly made his way to find her.

Aravind entered the living area and glanced at the two bedrooms on either side. Ravivaruman, understanding his son's search, gestured towards the left-side bedroom where Aravind's mother, Pallavi, was resting. Silently, Aravind made his way to her room.

As he entered, he saw his mother lying on the bed, her one side hand immobilized due to a stroke. Her face bore the signs of age and weariness, but there was still a glow of love and care in her eyes. Aravind sat down beside her, taking in her changed appearance and reminiscing about the past.

He remembered how his mother used to prepare his favourite dishes with so much love and how she always protected him from his father's sternness. Aravind had always been closest to his mother, cherishing her affectionate nature and unwavering support.

Now, seeing her in this state, tears welled up in Aravind's eyes. Pallavi, slightly awakening from her sleep, noticed her son's presence and smiled at him with all the warmth of an angel. Despite her own health struggles, her love for Aravind was unwavering.

Aravind, choked with emotion, asked his mother about her health. Pallavi's smile widened as she responded, her voice filled with love and reassurance. She assured Aravind that she was doing fine and expressed her happiness at seeing him. Their bond, strong as ever, brought a sense of comfort to Aravind's troubled heart.

Pallavi, still in bed, asked Aravind who his father was speaking with. Aravind explained that their grandchildren had arrived, and Pallavi's face lit up with joy, like waves flowing in the sea. Eager to see them, Pallavi attempted to get up from the wooden bed, but Aravind gently told her to wait while he went to fetch the kids.

In the hall, Aravind saw his father playing with his grandsons and felt a sense of awe. He couldn't help but wonder why his own father had never shown such warmth and affection towards him. Gathering his thoughts, Aravind approached his father and informed him that their mother wanted to see the children.

Ravivaruman, concerned about Pallavi's health, inquired if she had gotten up from her sleep. Assured by Aravind that she was awake, Ravivaruman urged his grandchildren to go and see their grandma. The children eagerly followed Aravind back to their grandmother's room, their excitement palpable in the air.

Aravind led his two children into his mother's room and introduced them to her. He explained that Sanjay was in the fourth standard while Amal corrected him, saying he was in Grade 1, not the first standard. Pallavi smiled at Amal's correction and lovingly called them both closer.

Aravind encouraged the children to go near their grandmother, and Pallavi hugged them tightly with one hand, tears of joy streaming down her face. Just then, Ravivaruman entered the room with hot water and soup for Pallavi, urging her to eat. However, Pallavi insisted that she would eat later, promising to do so soon. She then asked Ravivaruman to prepare food for the children, and he assured her that he had already ordered it.

Ravivaruman then turned to Aravind and suggested that he and the children freshen up after their long journey. Aravind nodded and led his sons out of the room to get cleaned up, leaving Pallavi and Ravivaruman together, sharing a moment of quiet affection.

Part 31

REDISCOVERING ROOTS

Aravind made sure the children freshened up, and then he went to take a bath himself. Meanwhile, Sanjay and Amal started to explore their grandmother's house together. Amal was full of energy, running around the house and exploring every corner, while Sanjay, being the responsible older brother, tried to keep him in check.

As they roamed around, Amal couldn't help but be captivated by the beauty of the garden. He ran towards the jackfruit tree and admired its large fruits, as well as the grapevines intertwined around it. Sanjay followed along, trying to keep pace with his brother.

In the backyard, they noticed two tall areca nut trees swaying in the breeze. The house was surrounded by a six-foot compound wall with an electric shock net on top for security.

Amal suddenly stopped and asked Sanjay if he could hear the sound. Sanjay initially didn't hear anything, but after Amal insisted, he focused and said he could hear the sound of a waterfall.

Curious, they both pressed their ears against the compound wall and listened intently to the soothing sound of water cascading down nearby.

After getting freshened up, Aravind called his children, and they quickly made their way to him. As they reached their father, there was a knock on the door, and a hotel staff member handed over the food ordered by Ravivaruman. The staff asked about Pallavi's health, and Ravivaruman assured them that she was doing fine.

Ravivaruman called Aravind to join them for food, and Aravind took the food to the dining table. He opened the parcel to reveal a variety of non-vegetarian dishes, including chicken fry, mutton masala, and crab, along with chicken soup.

Amal eagerly grabbed a piece of tandoori chicken and started to taste it, but Sanjay hesitated to eat. Seeing his reluctance, Aravind encouraged Sanjay to eat, but he still hesitated. It was only when Ravivaruman came into the dining hall and sat behind Sanjay, encouraging him to eat, that Sanjay finally started to eat.

Ravivaruman then poured some vegetable clear soup into a wooden bowl and took it to his wife, Pallavi. He started to feed her gently, and Aravind watched with mixed emotions. He couldn't help but notice the change in his father's behaviour towards his mother. It was a stark contrast to the strict and distant father he remembered from his childhood.

The sight of his father caring for his mother so tenderly made Aravind realize how much things had changed over the years. He felt a sense of gratitude for this small moment of warmth and care in their family.

After finishing dinner, Sanjay and Amal eagerly went with their grandfather Ravivaruman, discussing their studies along the way. Meanwhile, Aravind went to his mother's room and sat beside her, seeking comfort. He asked her about his father's changed behaviour and character.

Pallavi, Aravind's mother, replied softly, explaining that his father didn't know how to express love but was always a principled person. Aravind shared with his mother the fear that had plagued him from a young age until now, preventing him from standing up to his father. Tears welled up in his eyes as he expressed his pain.

Pallavi understood her son's suffering and comforted him with a smile, assuring him that time would bring change. Meanwhile, the sound of crackers filled the air, prompting Sanjay and Amal to ask their grandfather about the reason for the noise.

Ravivaruman explained to the boys that the crackers were being set off to scare away elephants from entering the town. This revelation sparked a mix of curiosity and fear in the children, who were fascinated by the idea of elephants but also wary of their potential danger.

Aravind couldn't help but notice the stark difference in his father's demeanour when talking to his grandchildren. He wished his father could speak to him with the same warmth and affection. Yet, despite his longing, he found solace in the love and understanding he shared with his mother.

Ravivaruman instructed his grandchildren to go and sleep, and they obediently headed to their respective rooms. Aravind stood in the living area, waiting for the children to come near him. Amal expressed his desire to sleep with their grandfather, but Aravind gently explained that their grandmother needed their grandfather's care, and they could play together tomorrow. Aravind then led the children to his bedroom.

The bedroom was adorned with books, and a bag hung on the wall caught Amal's attention. He pointed to it and asked Aravind what it was. Aravind smiled and replied that it was the first gift their mother, Tessy, had given him. Sanjay was intrigued by the bag's unique design and asked his father if he could make a call to his mom.

Aravind nodded and dialled Tessy's number. As the phone rang, Aravind's heart raced with anticipation. Tessy's phone started to ring, and Aravind's mind filled with thoughts of their past and the uncertainties of their future together.

Tessy lay in her bed feeling sorrowful after receiving the call from Aravind, but her mood brightened as she heard her children's voices on the other end. She attended the call, and Sanjay eagerly informed her that they had reached safely. He recounted all the naughty things Amal had been up to and how their grandfather had spoken with him, and their grandmother had cried.

Tessy asked to speak to Amal, but Sanjay explained that Amal was pretending to sleep. Despite feeling a pang of disappointment, Tessy told Sanjay to make sure Amal ate properly and took care of himself. Sanjay assured her and said goodbye, ending the call.

Tessy lay in bed, her thoughts drifting to her younger son. She hoped he would be okay and silently wished she could speak to him. Despite the distance and the challenges, they faced, her love for her children remained unwavering.

Part 32

MISTY MOUNTAINS AND JUNGLE ENCOUNTERS

Amal woke up at 6:30 and found his brother Sanjay sleeping peacefully. Feeling mischievous, Amal decided to wake him up by making some noise near his ear. Sanjay, startled, woke up with a jolt, his eyes wide with fear. Amal then darted off to the garden area, enticed by the mist-covered mountains in the distance. As he reached the garden, he was mesmerized by the beauty of the mist gently hitting the mountains. Amal opened his mouth in awe, watching as misty air escaped with his breath. Sanjay quickly followed suit, equally amazed by the scene before them.

Meanwhile, the servant named Baskar, with his long hair and moderate complexion, called out to Ravivaruman, informing him that a cheetah had been caught by the forest officers and there was no need to worry anymore. Ravivaruman calmly replied, advising Baskar not to disturb the animals, as they wouldn't disturb them either. With a smile, Baskar went about his work of cleaning the garden, occasionally exchanging words with the children.

Seeing the two boys, Baskar asked if they were Ravivaruman's grandsons. Sanjay proudly affirmed, and then asked about the wild animals in the area. Baskar replied that there were elephants, cheetahs, foxes, and even lions. Sanjay's eyes widened with excitement, and he eagerly asked if there were really lions around. Baskar admitted that while some people claimed to have seen lions, no one could confirm it. However, he mentioned a rumour that Aravind had seen a lion in his younger days.

Just then, Aravind called out to Sanjay and Amal. Amal started moving towards him eagerly, and Sanjay quickly followed suit, excited to join his father.

Aravind called out to his children to freshen up, informing them that they would be exploring various beautiful places that day. Sanjay and Aravind bathed and got ready. After finishing, Sanjay searched for his father and found him outside the house. With excitement, Sanjay called out, "Daddy!" Aravind, pleasantly surprised by the term "daddy," turned to Sanjay with a smile. He hugged Sanjay, but Sanjay, still curious, asked if Aravind had seen a lion.

Aravind chuckled and confirmed that he had indeed seen a lion. When Sanjay mentioned Baskar as the one who told him about the lion, Aravind's expression shifted slightly, but he quickly regained his composure and smiled. Baskar, sensing the tension, clarified that he had only mentioned it casually. Aravind smiled again, relieved.

Sanjay then expressed his desire to see a lion in the jungle, comparing it to seeing one in the zoo. He explained how he wanted to see the lion as the true king of the forest, walking majestically. Aravind understood Sanjay's wish and after some contemplation, he agreed. However, he cautioned Sanjay not to tell anyone, and they would have to observe the lion from a distance for safety.

Sanjay eagerly agreed, promising not to tell anyone. He was thrilled that his father had agreed to fulfil his wish to see the forest king.

Part 33

CLOSE CALLS AND COURAGE

After getting ready, Aravind gathered Sanjay and Amal, who were chatting with their grandmothers. Aravind informed his mother, Pallavi, that they were going out for an outing. Pallavi, with concern in her voice, insisted that Aravind take care of the children safely.

She pointed to a green box in front of her bed on the glass shelf and asked Aravind to bring it. Aravind fetched the box and handed it to his mother. Pallavi opened it with one hand, revealing bundles of Rs500, Rs100, and Rs200 notes inside. She took some money and gave it to Aravind, insisting that it was for their grandchildren.

Aravind smiled gratefully and accepted the money, thanking his mother. He then walked out with the children, Sanjay and Amal, who were excitedly chattering about the outing. They happily exclaimed to their grandfather, Ravivaruman, that they were going with daddy for an outing.

Ravivaruman advised Aravind to return home before evening, to which Aravind nodded in agreement. Aravind started the bike, and the children climbed on, ready for their adventure. With Sanjay and Amal seated behind him, Aravind began their journey, ready to explore the wonders of the surrounding area.

Aravind parked the bike near Beeman Falls and cautioned Amal not to run off too far. He assured him that he would join them soon. As they approached the falls, the sound of rushing water grew louder. Beeman Falls stood majestically, with water cascading down the hundred-foot rock face.

The children were thrilled to see the falls, especially Amal, who couldn't wait to jump into the water. Aravind reminded him to be careful and not go too deep. Sanjay, on the other hand, was disappointed that they hadn't seen the lion yet. He asked his father impatiently if they were going to see it soon.

Aravind smiled at Sanjay's eagerness and promised to take him to see the lion after they spent some time at the falls. He pointed out a small walking path beside the falls that led to another scenic spot. Sanjay's mood brightened at the prospect of seeing the lion, and he eagerly agreed to wait.

Meanwhile, Amal wasted no time and started removing his clothes to enjoy the water. He splashed around happily, laughing and giggling as he played in the shallow part of the falls. Aravind watched over them, making sure they were safe while enjoying the beauty of nature surrounding them.

As Amal splashed around, he turned to Aravind and asked, "Can we go deeper, Daddy?"

Aravind shook his head gently. "No, Amal. It's not safe to go deeper into the water."

As the family moved closer to the edge of the falls, Aravind noticed a separate path leading away from the main area. It looked partially closed off, but Aravind couldn't shake the feeling that someone might be watching them from the shadows.

"Come on, kids," Aravind said quietly, gesturing for them to follow him. "Let's go this way."

Amal quickly put on his clothes and joined his father and brother as they carefully made their way along the path. The sounds of insects filled the air, adding to the eerie atmosphere as they moved deeper into the forest.

Aravind kept a close eye on his children, making sure they stayed safe as they navigated the winding path. Finally, they reached a small clearing with a sandy dune overlooking surrounded by lush greenery.

"Wait here, kids," Aravind whispered. "I'm going to climb up and see if I can spot any lions. If it's safe, I'll call you up. Sanjay and Amal nodded; their eyes wide with anticipation as Aravind climbed the dune.

Aravind carefully climbed the small dune made of sand, moving quietly and making sure not to disturb anything. As he reached the top, he looked out over the landscape and spotted a large lake and on the other side deep forest, Deep in the forest, nestled amidst towering trees and dense foliage, lay a hidden cave. The entrance was partially concealed by vines and branches, adding to its mysterious allure. This cave was known as the King's Fort among the wild animals that inhabited the forest. Aravind's eyes scanned the area, searching for any signs of the lion.

Sanjay and Amal remained where they were, standing among the small trees, eagerly waiting for their father to return. Sanjay couldn't contain his excitement and asked Aravind if he had seen the lion yet. Aravind raised his hand, gesturing for Sanjay to wait.

Aravind continued to observe the other side of the lake intently, his eyes focused on every movement. Suddenly, he spotted something moving among the trees. It was the lion, majestic and powerful, blending into its surroundings with ease.

Aravind quietly signalled for Sanjay and Amal to come closer, but to remain silent. The children approached cautiously; their eyes wide with wonder as they caught sight of the lion across the lake.

Sanjay whispered excitedly, "There it is, Amal! The lion!" Amal's eyes widened in amazement as he watched the magnificent creature from a safe distance.

Sanjay, Amal, and their father Aravind stood at a safe distance, observing the majestic lion as it roamed gracefully through the wilderness. The lion's powerful presence commanded respect, and Sanjay couldn't help but feel awe-inspired by the sight.

With wide eyes and a beaming smile, Sanjay explained to Amal and his father, "See this, Amal? That's a lion. Look at the way it walks, so confidently, like a true king of the jungle."

Amal nodded in agreement; his eyes fixated on the lion's every move. He marvelled at its golden mane and the regal demeanour that seemed to exude from every step.

Aravind watched his sons with pride, appreciating their admiration for the wild beauty of nature. He smiled as Sanjay continued, "The lion's colour, its bravery, its face and its hair flowing in the hair —everything about it tells us that it's the real king of this world, even today."

As they stood there, mesmerized by the lion's presence, Aravind felt a sense of wonder at the wonders of nature. He knew that this experience would stay with his sons forever, teaching them the importance of respect and appreciation for the world around them.

Aravind stood silently, taking in the sight with his children. It was a moment of pure awe and admiration for the beauty and grace of the king of the jungle. After a while, Aravind gently led his children back down the hill, their hearts still racing with the thrill of the encounter.

As they were returning from the place, Sanjay was filled with excitement from having seen the lion. He expressed his desire to see it again, but his excitement turned to fear when they encountered a large black bull waiting in their path.

Sanjay screamed in fear, but Aravind quickly reacted, placing Amal in a safe spot and reassuring Sanjay that he was with him. Aravind knew he had to act fast, so he called out to the bull in a manner that people in Tamil Nadu often use during "jallikattu," a traditional bull-taming sport that dates back thousands of years.

Aravind urged Sanjay to slowly move away from the bull, trying to keep the situation under control. However, the bull started to charge towards Sanjay. Aravind, without hesitation, shouted loudly and made noise to distract the bull. He positioned himself between the bull and his son, ready to face the danger head-on.

The bull charged at Aravind with full force, but he managed to grab onto its neck and steer it away from Sanjay. With all his strength, Aravind guided the bull towards a nearby lake. As they reached the edge of the water, the bull slipped and fell into the lake, momentarily stunned.

Aravind quickly ushered his children away from the danger, urging them to run. They sprinted towards safety as fast as they could, with the sound of the raging bull behind them.

Despite the bull managing to get back on its feet and charging towards them once again, Aravind and his children reached the waterfall's edge just in time. They plunged into the water, escaping the bull's attack.

As they emerged from the water, Aravind felt a sense of relief wash over him. Sanjay, realizing the danger they had narrowly escaped, hugged his father tightly and kissed his cheeks, tears of gratitude in his eyes. He told Aravind how much he loved him, appreciating his father's bravery and protection. Aravind hugged him back, feeling the warmth of their bond, knowing that no matter what dangers they faced, they would always have each other's love and support.

Part 34

BACK TO REALITY

Day 3 dawned with Aravind preparing to leave Jamunamaruthar and return to Chennai. Meanwhile, in Pallavi's room, she and Ravivaruman were enjoying their time with their grandchildren, sharing smiles and laughter. Aravind couldn't help but admire the happiness on his mother's face as he glanced at their wedding photo hanging on the wall.

Sanjay entered Pallavi's room, his innocent request to his grandmother to come with them tugging at her heartstrings. Tears welled up in Pallavi's eyes as she realized the depth of her grandson's affection.

Ravivaruman, sensing the sombre mood, asked Aravind if he could extend his leave. Aravind stood in silence, unable to fulfil his father's request. Amal chimed in, reminding his grandfather that the court had allowed only three days for the visit.

Understanding the situation, Ravivaruman advised Aravind to get started on their journey back to Chennai as soon as possible. With a heavy heart, Aravind sat beside his mother, pleading for her to come with them. But Pallavi gently refused, and Aravind had to accept her decision, despite his longing to take care of her.

As they bid farewell to their grandparents, Sanjay and Amal showered them with kisses, their hearts heavy with the weight of leaving. Amal, smiling, settled in front of the bike, while Sanjay couldn't shake the feeling of sadness, missing the love and warmth of their grandparents already.

With a final goodbye, Aravind started the bike, and they began their journey back to the city. Sanjay couldn't help but feel a pang of longing as they left behind the natural beauty of Jamunamaruthar, carrying with him cherished memories of their time spent with their beloved grandparents.

As Aravind and the children returned to Chennai, the noise and chaos of the city greeted them. Sanjay couldn't help but feel overwhelmed by the contrast between the serene beauty of his grandparents' home and the hustle and bustle of Chennai's streets. The air was thick with pollution, and the constant honking of vehicles filled the atmosphere.

Aravind stopped the bike in Vandalur, a bustling area on the outskirts of Chennai. Sanjay sighed, missing the tranquillity of the forest and the warmth of his grandparents' home. Aravind, feeling his son's disappointment, decided to call Tessy to inform her of their arrival.

Tessy answered the phone, her voice distracted as she spoke to her colleagues about work. Aravind informed her that they had reached Vandalur and asked when she would be able to meet them. Tessy, caught up in her work responsibilities, replied that she would come later and instructed Aravind to drop the children off at the apartments.

Aravind felt a pang of sadness at Tessy's response. He longed for the comfort and support of his family, especially after the peaceful time they had spent in Jamunamaruthar. Despite his disappointment, he knew he had to fulfil his responsibilities as a father and ensure the children's safety. With a heavy heart, he agreed to Tessy's plan and focused on getting the children safely home.

Aravind reached the apartments with Sanjay and Amal, but Sanjay hesitated to leave his father's side so soon. He wanted more time with him. Suddenly, Sanjay complained of hunger, prompting Aravind to decide to buy some snacks. He asked Amal what he wanted, and Amal requested a butterscotch milkshake, saying his stomach wasn't feeling well.

At 6:20 PM, Aravind checked his phone and realized it was time for Tessy's arrival. Amal eagerly started drinking his milkshake, but Sanjay ate slowly, feeling unhappy about being separated from his father.

At 6:25 PM, Tessy arrived at the apartment and inquired about the boys to Peter, the watchman. He informed her that they were eating in the cafeteria. Tessy entered the cafeteria and thanked Aravind for taking care of the children. Aravind smiled and Tessy told she could take over now. Aravind silently moved away, but Sanjay watched with a heavy heart and Amal cried for his father as he left.

Tessy managed to comfort Amal, while Sanjay sat in the cafeteria, his eyes filled with tears. As Aravind started his motorcycle, the sound of his Royal Enfield echoed outside. Sanjay listened to the familiar sound, feeling the weight of his father's absence. He wiped away his tears, hoping for the day when he could spend more time with his dad.

Part - 35

THE REALITIES

*I*n the Ascends Infotainment Soft IT Park, on the third floor, a conference hall meeting was in progress. Aravind, the team leader, sat among other team leaders, looking dishevelled with an unkempt beard, speckled with both white and black hairs. His glasses were smudged, and his attire, a white shirt and light brown pants, seemed hastily put together, lacking proper ironing.

The meeting commenced with the manager discussing project reports and team performances. Arun Kumar was praised for his outstanding performance in a difficult project, while several other team leaders were acknowledged as well. However, the atmosphere grew tense when the manager expressed frustration over Aravind's team's performance, citing numerous bugs and escalations.

Aravind remained silent throughout the manager's criticism, his expression stoic and unmoved. Priya Sharma, a colleague who had clashed with Aravind in the past, couldn't hide her satisfaction at seeing him face trouble in the office.

As the meeting concluded, Aravind quietly exited the conference room and retreated to his cabin. He sat at his desk, contemplating the manager's words. His phone rang, displaying the name of the

Human Resources (HR) department. With a heavy sigh, Aravind answered the call, expecting to discuss the issues raised in the meeting and perhaps even his own performance.

On the other side of the phone, the HR head instructed Aravind to come to the HR department for a meeting at 4 o'clock. Aravind acknowledged the message and agreed to attend.

At 4:30 pm, Aravind arrived at the HR department and entered the room of Mr. Deepak, the Head of Human Resource Department. The HR room was adorned with glass doors and had Deepak's name prominently displayed. Deepak, with a fresh and composed demeanour, welcomed Aravind with a smile.

Aravind sat silently as Deepak began discussing his performance over the past year. Deepak pointed out that Aravind's performance had not been up to the mark and that the management was not satisfied. Despite giving several chances for improvement, Aravind had not shown any significant progress.

Aravind listened quietly, without arguing or showing any signs of anger. He knew that what Deepak was saying was correct. After some contemplation, Deepak mentioned that higher-level management was considering termination, but he suggested resignation instead.

Deepak explained that resignation would be a better option for Aravind as it would save face and potentially allow him to find a new job without the stigma of termination. Despite feeling disappointed, Deepak reassured Aravind that he was talented and would likely find opportunities elsewhere.

Aravind smiled, understanding the nature of corporate decisions and human resources. He agreed to submit his resignation, acknowledging the inevitability of the situation. He expressed his gratitude to Deepak and assured him that he would comply with the decision.

With a sense of resignation, Aravind left the HR cabin, contemplating his next steps and the uncertainty of his future.

Part 36

THE HAPPY SPACE

At exactly 7:30 PM, Aravind sat at the Happy Space Liquor Bar in Navalur, holding a glass filled with vodka. His phone rang, and it was his friend Mugilan on the line. With slurred speech, Aravind spoke into the phone, "Hey, Mugilan! I'm at the Happy Space Liquor Bar in Navalur. I've already finished half a bottle of vodka, and there's more to go! I also have some vodka lemon flavour near my table, but I haven't touched the snacks yet."

As Aravind continued his conversation, his speech was increasingly difficult to understand due to the effects of the alcohol. After completing his slurred speech, he hung up the phone and sat back in his chair. His head was spinning, and he struggled to focus on his surroundings.

The bar was bustling with activity, with people ordering their favourite drinks and enjoying themselves at the long lounge tables. The colourful lighting and vibrant atmosphere of the bar only added to Aravind's sense of disorientation.

Despite feeling unstable and unable to stand properly, Aravind remained seated, his gaze drifting aimlessly around the bar. The effects of the liquor were becoming more pronounced, and he found it difficult to concentrate on anything besides the swirling colours and sounds around him.

Within a short while, Mugilan arrived at the Happy Space Lounge Bar and called Aravind's mobile, but there was no response. He scanned the crowded bar, searching for his friend, but couldn't spot him at first. After a moment, he noticed Aravind sitting alone in a corner, his gaze fixed on the lively scene before him.

With the background music blasting and people chatting and laughing, Mugilan made his way over to Aravind. As he approached, Aravind looked up and greeted him with a smile. "Hey, Mugilan! Glad you could make it," Aravind said, his speech slightly slurred from the drinks.

Mugilan, dressed in his formal attire with polished shoes, chuckled and replied, "Yeah, one friend is enough to pull me away from work."

Aravind gestured for Mugilan to take a seat beside him, and Mugilan settled in, taking in the vibrant atmosphere of the bar. "How's it going, Aravind?" Mugilan asked, noticing the half-empty glass of vodka on the table.

Aravind shrugged, his eyes still fixed on the colourful lights and bustling activity around them. "Just enjoying the vibes, you know," he replied, his words slightly muddled.

Mugilan sighed inwardly, realizing that Aravind had probably had a bit too much to drink. "Well, as long as you're having a good time," Mugilan said, trying to keep the conversation light.

As the night wore on, Mugilan stayed by Aravind's side, making sure his friend was okay amidst the lively chaos of the bar.

Mugilan was munching on the snacks that Aravind had bought when Aravind smiled and made a remark, "One thing that hasn't changed is you, Mugilan."

Curious, Mugilan asked, "What's up, buddy?"

Aravind, his speech slightly slurred from the alcohol, opened up about his recent struggles. "I've lost my focus at work. Today, HR gave me the option to either resign or face termination," he confessed. "But I've already applied for resignation. I'm not worried about that."

Mugilan felt a pang of concern for his friend. "I'm sorry to hear that, Aravind," he said, feeling uneasy about the situation.

Aravind, with tears welling up in his eyes, continued, "I've also lost my wife and children's. I neglected them because I was too focused on settling in the UK or USA."

Mugilan stopped eating, feeling saddened by Aravind's words. He watched as Aravind wiped his tears away with both hands. "Don't worry, buddy," Aravind reassured him. "I've accepted the pain now. It doesn't hurt as much anymore."

As Aravind continued to share his worries, Mugilan made a decision. He knew he had to do something to help his friend. While Aravind reached for another bottle of vodka, mixing it with soft drinks, Mugilan discreetly made a call to Mr. Gulam Nabi Azad, Aravind's advocate, and scheduled an appointment for the next day.

The background music continued to blare, and the crowd at the bar remained lively, but Mugilan couldn't shake off the feeling of concern for his friend. He hoped that the appointment with the advocate would bring some clarity and help Aravind through this tough time.

Part 37

SEEKING RESOLUTION

Aravind and Mugilan sat outside the waiting hall next to the name board of Mr. Gulam Nabi Azad, MA., LLB, Advocate. Aravind observed the numerous people waiting there and Mugilan, trying to lighten the mood, asked, "Are all these people waiting for divorces nowadays?" He chuckled, adding, "Seems like people are filing for divorce even before they get married!" Aravind, however, didn't find it amusing. He shot Mugilan a glare, his irritation evident.

Mugilan fell silent, sensing Aravind's mood, and they waited quietly. After a while, a young practicing lawyer came out and called Aravind's name. Aravind and Mugilan entered Gulam's office, where the advocate greeted them with a warm smile.

"Good morning, Mr. Aravind. Good morning, Mr. Mugilan. Please have a seat," said Gulam, gesturing towards the chairs opposite his desk.

Aravind and Mugilan sat down; Mugilan explained to Advocate Gulam the current situation Aravind was facing due to his family issues. Aravind interjected, expressing his struggle with concentration and confidence, admitting that he had lost all hope. He felt directionless and unsure of what to do next.

Mugilan then asked Advocate Gulam if there was any chance of reconciling Aravind and Tessy's relationship, pleading for his help to overcome the situation. Gulam listened intently, his fingers pressed against his head as he contemplated the best course of action.

After a moment of deep thought, Gulam addressed Aravind with a serious expression. "Aravind, will you cooperate with me? Can you handle the steps I plan to take?" he asked.

Aravind nodded, though he seemed apprehensive. "Yes, I will cooperate. But please, don't emotionally hurt my wife. She's already going through a lot," he said, his voice filled with concern for Tessy.

Gulam responded firmly, "Sometimes, breaking down emotions is necessary to rebuild. But rest assured, I will handle it in a way that won't harm her. Trust me, it's for the best."

Aravind remained silent, deep in thought, while Mugilan nodded in agreement. "Whatever we have to face, we'll face it together," he affirmed, offering his support to his friend.

Advocate Gulam nodded, formulating a plan in his mind. He knew he had to tread carefully to navigate the complexities of Aravind and Tessy's relationship. With determination and a strategic approach, he was confident he could help them find a resolution.

Part 38

RISING STAR CRICKET CLUB

*T*essy sat on the bleachers of the school playground, watching the intense cricket match unfold on the pitch. Beside her, Amal sat eagerly, his eyes fixed on the players. Today was Sanjay and Amal's school sports day, and although Amal wasn't participating in the sports events as he was below the age limit, he was excited to watch his brother and the other children compete.

The final match was between Junior Thunderbolts and Rising Stars Cricket Club. Both teams were displaying excellent skills, wearing their white cricket jerseys with pride. The scoreboard showed that Junior Thunderbolts had scored 102/6 runs in their 15 overs, while Rising Stars Cricket Club was currently playing and had scored 66/7, having already lost seven wickets.

Sanjay, who was part of the Junior Thunderbolts team, had contributed 12 runs off 10 balls, while Arjun had only managed to score 1 run off 6 balls. As the match progressed into the middle of the 9th over, the tension on the field was palpable.

The bowler from Junior Thunderbolts sent the ball hurtling towards the batsman from Rising Stars Cricket Club. With precision and skill, the batsman managed to connect, sending the ball soaring across the field. The fielders from Junior Thunderbolts scrambled to stop it, but the batsmen managed to score a couple of runs before the ball was returned.

Tessy cheered along with the other parents, her heart pounding with excitement. She glanced at Amal, who was clapping enthusiastically, his eyes sparkling with admiration for his brother and the other players.

Tessy sat on the bleachers of the school playground; her eyes fixed on the cricket match unfolding before her. It was the final match of the school sports day, and her son Sanjay was playing for the Rising Stars Cricket Club. Beside her, her youngest son Amal sat, his head nodding as he dozed off.

The atmosphere was tense as the Junior Thunderbolts had set a challenging target of 102 runs in 15 overs. Now, with Rising Stars Cricket Club at 66/7 in the 9th over, the pressure was on. Sanjay, her elder son, had scored 12 runs off 10 balls, while his partner Arjun was struggling at 1 run off 6 balls.

Sanjay was determined to lead his team to victory. He started to show his skills, placing the ball cleverly in different areas of the field with precise shots - leg side, off side, and square cuts. With his strategic play, he managed to bring the score to 89 runs in 14 overs.

As the last over began, the situation was critical. Fourteen runs were needed from six balls. Tessy watched intently as Sanjay took his position at the crease. The first ball was a defensive shot, leaving five balls to get 14 runs.

On the second ball, Sanjay managed to get a thick edge, and the ball raced to the boundary for a four. The required runs reduced to ten from four balls. The tension mounted as Sanjay faced the third ball.

With a determined swing, Sanjay smashed the ball for a six, bringing the target down to just four runs from three balls. The crowd erupted into cheers, giving him a standing ovation.

The next ball was a yorker, leaving Sanjay unable to score. With just two balls left and four runs to win, the pressure was immense. Sanjay played defensively, hoping to keep his wicket intact.

It all came down to the last ball. Sanjay faced the bowler, his heart pounding. The bowler delivered a good ball, but Sanjay struck it perfectly, sending it flying to the offside for a boundary. The crowd erupted into wild cheers as Rising Stars Cricket Club won the match.

Tessy couldn't contain her joy as she cheered for her son, her heart swelling with pride. Sanjay's teammates lifted him on their shoulders, celebrating his heroic innings. Even Amal, who had woken up from his sleep, clapped sleepily, sensing the excitement around him.

Part 39

THE TROPHY OF TRIUMPH

As the cricket match came to an exhilarating end, the presentation ceremony began. Sister Rachel, a revered figure in the school who had been there since its founding 30 years ago, sat in her chair, her age evident in her frailty. Yet, her spirit remained strong as ever.

When Sanjay's name was announced as the Man of the Match, Sister Rachel's face lit up with a warm smile. With a gentle gesture, she blessed him, placing her finger on his head. Sanjay, filled with pride and gratitude, approached Sister Rachel to receive his award.

The trophy was a medium-sized masterpiece, adorned with golden and silver hues. At the top, an intricately crafted eagle soared, symbolizing victory and achievement. Sanjay accepted the trophy with a beaming smile, his eyes shining with joy and accomplishment.

His friends surrounded him, cheering and clapping as they celebrated their victory. Sanjay held the trophy high, feeling a sense of triumph and satisfaction wash over him. Tessy, watching from the sidelines, felt her heart swell with pride. As a single mother, seeing her son achieve such success filled her with immense happiness and fulfilment.

Sanjay's achievement was not just a win for him but a testament to Tessy's dedication and hard work in raising her children. She wiped away tears of joy as she watched her son bask in the glory of his accomplishment. In that moment, she knew that all the sacrifices she had made were worth it.

Sanjay proudly approached his mother, Tessy, with the trophy in hand. As he reached her, Amal eagerly snatched the trophy from Sanjay's grasp, but Sanjay brushed him off and handed the trophy to Tessy. Tessy accepted the trophy with a smile, but she immediately passed it to Amal, knowing how much he wanted to show it off to his friends.

Amal gleefully ran off to show the trophy to his classmates, while Tessy and Sanjay walked over to a nearby sitting area. Tessy praised Sanjay's performance, telling him how great his match was and how awesome his winning moment looked.

However, Tessy couldn't help but express her concerns to Sanjay about his gameplay. She pointed out how he consistently made wrong shots, despite having opportunities for better ones. Tessy emphasized the importance of footwork and stability in cricket, urging Sanjay to improve in these areas.

Sanjay listened quietly, absorbing his mother's feedback. He defended his performance, insisting that he had played correctly.

But Tessy remained firm in her observations, reminding him of the importance of concentration and consistency.

Realizing that his mother only wanted the best for him, Sanjay finally nodded in agreement. He acknowledged his areas for improvement and promised to work on them in upcoming matches. Sanjay smiled, appreciating his mother's guidance and support.

Meanwhile, Amal returned to Tessy with the trophy, eager to get it back. He forcefully snatched it from her, excited to continue showing it off to his friends. Tessy chuckled at Amal's enthusiasm, grateful for her sons' joys and the bond they shared as a family.

After a delightful time spent with her children, Sanjay and Amal, Tessy arrived at her apartment complex around 4:30 pm. As they entered the gate, the watchman, Peter, greeted Tessy as "madam" and handed her a registered post. Tessy thanked him and proceeded towards the cafeteria with her children in an auto.

The cafeteria was renowned for its evening snacks, and Tessy decided to treat her children for their excellent performance at the sports day. She told Sanjay and Amal they could have whatever they wanted. Excitedly, Amal rushed towards the glass box containing various junk foods like samosas and puffs. He carefully selected a variety of items, while Sanjay opted for a samosa.

Tessy made the payment using digital GPay, scanning the QR code with her phone. With the snacks in hand, they found a table to sit and enjoy their treats. As the children began to eat, Tessy opened the registered post, only to find it was from the Guindy family court. Her heart sank as she read that Aravind had filed a new petition, and the court date was set for the coming Monday.

Feeling a wave of anxiety, Tessy immediately called her advocate to discuss the matter. She explained the situation and asked for guidance on how to proceed. The advocate reassured Tessy and promised to handle the matter with utmost care. Despite the sudden setback, Tessy remained determined to face the challenges head-on for the sake of her children.

Part 40

THE COURTROOM CONFRONTATION

NOVEMBER 4TH 2019

Monday morning at 8:00 am, Tessy called her children's class in charge to inform them about the leave for Sanjay and Amal. The class in charge, with a hint of annoyance, reminded Tessy about her children's frequent absences and requested her to reconsider. Tessy felt guilty, realizing that too many leaves could affect her children's education.

Struggling to find a taxi through the mobile app due to the morning rush, Tessy decided to step out of the apartment and hailed an auto, although the fare was higher than usual. She knew that Mondays were always hectic and time was crucial to cover the distance.

In the auto, Tessy called her office to request for leave, explaining her situation to the HR department. Understanding her predicament, they granted her permission for the day off.

The Courtroom Confrontation

Relieved, Tessy settled into the auto with Sanjay and Amal, move to Guindy Family Court.

Tessy met Ramya in her office, which was conveniently located near the court premises. Ramya warmly welcomed Tessy, understanding her situation well. Ramya had always believed in resolving conflicts amicably, encouraging couples to choose their path when problems arose. Her upbringing, witnessing her parents' constant fighting, had shaped her perspective, making her stand up for women's rights and needs.

As Tessy entered Ramya's office with her children, she appeared tense and worried. Tessy poured out her concerns about the ongoing petition from Aravind and the difficulties she faced in managing her job and family.

Ramya listened attentively, her eyes fixed on the vintage clock on the wall, its hands moving in two directions, indicating the passing time. It was 9:45 am. Despite not having all the details, Ramya assured Tessy that they would fight this time if needed.

Ramya's resolve to support Tessy was unwavering. She acknowledged Tessy's struggles and assured her that they would work together to tackle the situation. With a sense of determination, Ramya suggested they move to the court to address the matter head-on.

Advocate Ramya entered the courtroom with a sense of determination, her stride purposeful as she made her way to the designated area for attorneys. A group of advocates was already seated at the table, engaged in conversations and reviewing case files. Ramya exchanged nods with a few familiar faces before taking her seat among them.

Meanwhile, Tessy waited anxiously outside the courtroom with Sanjay and Amal, her mind filled with worry about the proceedings inside. The clock struck 10:00 am, and the respected Judge Mr. G. Govindraju arrived, commanding the attention of everyone present. As the judge took his seat on the elevated platform, the entire courtroom rose in respect before settling back down.

Judge Mr. G. Govindraju had a demeanour that exuded authority and fairness, known for his constant dedication to delivering proper judgments, he was respected by both advocates and litigants. His approachable nature made him popular among people seeking justice, especially in family court matters.

Behind the judge stood the mace-bearer, a symbol of authority, ready to enforce the judge's orders if necessary. The court assistants, seated below the judge's platform, were responsible for managing case files and assisting the judge during the proceedings.

As the court session began, the case files were called out by the judge's assistants, summoning the concerned parties to present their arguments. Inside the courtroom, Ramya prepared to represent Tessy's interests, determined to seek justice for her client.

As Aravind entered the courtroom with his Advocate, Gulam, Tessy couldn't help but feel a surge of anxiety. She glanced nervously at her children, Sanjay and Amal, who were standing beside her. Sanjay offered a hesitant smile, but he remained by his mother's side, sensing her unease.

The Courtroom Confrontation

On the other hand, Amal's face lit up as soon as he saw his father. With excitement, he rushed towards Aravind and enveloped him in a tight hug. Tessy's heart sank as she watched her younger son embrace his father. It was a bittersweet moment for her - seeing the bond between father and son, yet feeling the pain of their separation.

Aravind returned Amal's hug warmly, his expression softening as he embraced his son. He then looked towards Tessy, but she avoided making eye contact with him. It had been a long time since they had spoken or even acknowledged each other directly.

Feeling the tension in the air, Aravind gently guided Amal back to Tessy's side. He attempted to offer a reassuring smile, but Tessy remained distant, turning away from him. She couldn't bring herself to face him, not after everything that had transpired between them.

As the court proceedings began, Tessy focused her attention on her Advocate, Ramya. She trusted Ramya to represent her interests and fight for the best possible outcome. Meanwhile, Aravind sat across the courtroom, listening attentively to Advocate arguments in courtroom.

Despite the turmoil and emotions swirling inside her, Tessy remained composed, determined to navigate through the legal proceedings for the sake of her children. But deep down, the presence of Aravind in the same courtroom stirred up a mix of conflicting emotions within her.

Part 41

TESSY'S TOUGH CHOICE

At exactly 11:00 am, the case hearing for Aravind and Tessy began. The judge's assistant handed the petition filed by Gulam to the judge, and both Aravind and Tessy stood with their respective Advocates.

Tessy's advocate, Ramya, stood behind her, ready to represent her client's interests. Tessy stood with her children beside her, trying to stay composed despite the tension in the courtroom.

As the proceedings started, the judge signalled for Gulam to proceed with explaining the petition. However, before Gulam could start, Ramya interjected, addressing the judge.

"Your Honor, before we proceed, I would like to bring to your attention the struggles my client faces to attend these hearings," Ramya said, gesturing towards Tessy. "She has to manage her children and navigate through various challenges just to be present here."

The judge listened attentively, nodding in understanding. However, before Ramya could continue, the judge interrupted, wanting to hear from Aravind first.

"Let's first understand the reason behind this petition," the judge said, addressing Aravind directly. "Mr. Aravind, please proceed."

Aravind's Advocate, Gulam, stepped forward and began to explain the grounds for the petition.

Aravind's Advocate addressed the judge, "My Lord, my client is ready to give divorce. He has been struggling for four years, facing numerous challenges in his life, and now he believes divorce is the best solution."

Aravind stood silently beside his advocate, his face reflecting a mix of sorrow and resignation. Tessy, hearing the news, felt a wave of relief wash over her. Finally, after years of uncertainty and emotional turmoil, there seemed to be a resolution in sight.

For Tessy, this announcement meant the end of a long and difficult chapter in her life. She had endured countless struggles and hardships, but now, with Aravind's willingness to divorce, it seemed like a weight had been lifted off her shoulders. No longer would she have to endure the pain of seeing Aravind, or deal with the constant battles and conflicts in their relationship.

As the realization sunk in, Tessy felt a sense of liberation. She could now move forward with her life, focusing on herself and her children without the constant reminder of her failed marriage. It was a new beginning, filled with hope and possibilities.

With the prospect of divorce on the horizon, Tessy looked towards the future with optimism, knowing that she could finally start a new and build a better life for herself and her children.

Aravind's Advocate, Gulam, put forward a surprising condition: Aravind requested custody of one of the children because he felt hopeless and helpless. This unexpected condition left Tessy's advocate, Ramya, taken aback, as she hadn't anticipated such a request.

The judge, noticing Tessy's silence, called upon her for her opinion. Tessy stood in front of the judge, feeling a whirlwind of emotions. She was caught off guard by Aravind's request and was unsure of how to respond.

With a lump in her throat, Tessy struggled to find the right words. She glanced at her children, Sanjay and Amal, standing beside her, their innocent faces reflecting her own confusion and anxiety. How could she possibly choose between them? They were both her world, and the mere thought of being separated from either of them tore her apart.

Tessy's mind raced as she grappled with the weight of the decision before her. On one hand, she faced lot of pain because of Aravind but on the other hand, she couldn't bear the thought of losing custody of one of her beloved children.

As the silence stretched on, Tessy's heart sank. She felt overwhelmed and paralyzed by the choice she was being forced to make. In that moment, all she wanted was for this nightmare to end, for her family to be whole again, but it seemed like an impossible dream.

Finally, Tessy turned to her Advocate, Ramya, seeking guidance. Ramya, sensing Tessy's turmoil, whispered words of encouragement and support. With a deep breath, Tessy gathered her strength and addressed the judge.

"Your Honor," Tessy began, her voice trembling slightly, "I... I need some time to think about this. It's not an easy decision to make, and I want to do what's best for my children."

The judge nodded understandingly, granting Tessy the time and put next hearing for next month. she needed to consider her response. As Tessy left the courtroom with her children, her mind raced with conflicting thoughts and emotions. She knew she had a difficult road ahead, but she was determined to make the right choice for her family, no matter how challenging it might be.

As Aravind and his Advocate, Gulam, walked through the court premises, Gulam offered some words of reassurance. "Great things will happen soon, so don't worry," he said, trying to uplift Aravind's spirits. "In my point of view, Ramya will come up with a great plan. We will fight," he added confidently.

Aravind, though appreciative of Gulam's support, felt a mixture of hope and helplessness. On one hand, he held onto the hope that things might finally start to turn around for him. After years of struggles and uncertainties, the prospect of a resolution to his marital issues brought a glimmer of optimism.

Part 42

NAVIGATING CUSTODY BATTLES

As Tessy waited anxiously in Advocate Ramya's office, she watched her children playing outside, trying to distract herself from the weight of the situation. Sanjay kept a close eye on Amal, who was growing increasingly irritated by his brother's constant attention.

When Advocate Ramya finally emerged from her office, Tessy could see the tension in her expression. Ramya approached Tessy with a heavy heart, knowing the difficulty of the situation they were facing.

Tessy's eyes were filled with tears as she confronted Ramya. "Is he really such a heartless person?" she asked, her voice trembling with emotion. "How can he be ready to separate our children just for his own needs?"

Ramya listened empathetically, understanding the depth of Tessy's pain. She reassured Tessy that they would do everything in their power to fight for her and her children's rights.

"I've never seen such a ridiculous man in my life," Tessy continued, her frustration evident in her voice. "To think that he would be willing to tear our family apart just to satisfy his own desires..."

Ramya placed a comforting hand on Tessy's shoulder, offering her support. "I know it's difficult, Tessy," she said softly. "But we will fight for what's right. We won't let him get away with this."

Tessy nodded, grateful for Ramya's reassurance. Despite the pain and uncertainty, she knew she had a strong advocate by her side who was determined to help her navigate through this challenging time.

As Tessy spoke with Advocate Ramya, she began to feel a glimmer of hope. Ramya's reassuring words and determination to fight for her gave Tessy some comfort amid the chaos.

"I think they have a plan," Ramya said confidently. "But we'll fight them every step of the way."

Ramya began asking Tessy some investigative questions to understand the situation better. "What's their demand?" she asked.

"They want me to hand over one child to Aravind," Tessy replied, her voice filled with frustration.

Ramya nodded; her expression thoughtful. "We're almost near to divorce," she explained. "They've submitted affidavits for mutual divorce, so our path is clear."

Tessy's heart skipped a beat at the news. It seemed like there was finally a way out of this difficult situation. Ramya continued; her tone eager. "We can agree to give them one child, but when the judge asks the children, they need to support living with you. That's when the case will be finished."

Tessy felt a surge of relief washes over her. Ramya had shown her a clear path forward, and Tessy couldn't help but feel grateful for her guidance.

Just then, Sanjay entered Advocate Ramya's room, a look of concern on his face. "Mom," he said urgently, "Amal is pouring water on the floor!"

Tessy sighed, a small smile tugging at the corners of her lips. Even amid their turmoil, her children still found ways to bring a sense of normalcy and humour to their lives. She knew that with Ramya by her side and her children's unwavering support, they would get through this challenging time together.

As Tessy prepared to scold Amal for his mischievous behaviour, Advocate Ramya quickly intervened, urging her to reconsider. "No, Tessy, it's not a good idea to scold him," she advised gently. Tessy sighed and reluctantly sat back down; her frustration still evident.

Ramya calmly reassured Tessy, "Sanjay will take care of Amal. Let's focus on what we can control."

Tessy nodded, her mind racing with thoughts. "I forget to tell you, she began, "Sanjay always says he'll stay with me, but Amal is different. He's always leaning towards his father."

Advocate Ramya listened intently; her expression sympathetic. "I understand, Tessy. But don't worry, you have a month's gap now. This is the best time to make a change. Take the opportunity to slowly influence Amal's mindset. His father won't be around every day."

Tessy mulled over Ramya's words, feeling conflicted but hopeful. She knew it wouldn't be easy to change Amal's perspective, but she was willing to try, especially with Ramya's guidance.

"Thank you, Ramya," Tessy said, her voice filled with gratitude. "I'll do my best."

With Ramya's encouragement and support, Tessy felt a renewed sense of determination. She knew that even though the road ahead would be challenging, she had someone by her side who believed in her and was ready to help her navigate the difficult journey ahead.

Part 43

REFLECTIONS ON UNCERTAINTY

As Tessy busied herself in the kitchen, she thought about the crucial month ahead. She knew that this time was vital for her and her children's future. Determined to make the most of it, she decided to start the day on a positive note by cooking Amal's favourite breakfast – an egg sandwich with cheese and French fries.

Meanwhile, Sanjay was getting ready for school, but he noticed that Amal wasn't putting on his uniform. Concerned about being late, Sanjay took charge and forcefully dressed Amal, who protested loudly.

Hearing the commotion, Tessy entered the room with a calm demeanour. "Sanjay, don't force Amal," she said gently. "Let him take his time. He'll understand."

With a softer approach, Tessy turned to Amal and spoke lovingly, "Amal, please get ready soon. I've prepared your favourite breakfast – egg sandwich and French fries."

Upon hearing the mention of his favourite dishes, Amal's face lit up, and he quickly got dressed and made his way to the dining table, eager to enjoy his breakfast.

Tessy smiled, relieved to see Amal responding positively. She knew that these small gestures of love and understanding were crucial in building a stronger bond with her son during this critical time.

Tessy sat in her cabin, deeply engrossed in analysing her team's performance when her office email pinged, Tessy's heart sank as she read the email notification of the layoffs at Coretronix Techno Solutions. She couldn't believe that her team member Karthick was on the list. Without wasting a moment, Tessy called the HR department to inquire about the sudden layoff.

The HR representative explained that the decision came from the head office and was affecting branches worldwide. It was a massive layoff, and the reasons behind it were not clear even to the HR department.

Feeling a mix of shock and concern, Tessy sat back in her chair, trying to process the news. She knew Karthick had been a dedicated member of their team, always putting in his best effort. The thought of him losing his job so suddenly was distressing.

As the news spread, the atmosphere in the office became tense. Colleagues whispered to each other, worried about their own positions. Tessy felt a sense of responsibility towards her team, knowing that she had to do something to support them during this difficult time.

She immediately scheduled a meeting with her team to discuss the situation and reassure them. Tessy wanted to provide them with as much information and support as possible, even though the situation was beyond her control.

Throughout the day, Tessy couldn't shake off the feeling of unease. The uncertainty of the layoffs lingered in her mind, making it difficult to focus on her work. She found herself constantly checking her phone for updates and hoping for some clarity on the situation.

As the day went on, Tessy realized that the layoffs were a harsh reminder of the volatile nature of the corporate world. She vowed to support her team through this challenging time and do whatever she could to help them navigate the uncertainty ahead.

As the evening descended, Karthick entered Tessy's cabin with a heavy heart. Tessy sat there; her face clouded with sorrow as she processed the news of the layoff. Upon seeing Karthick, she welcomed him, but her concern deepened as she noticed the change in his demeanour.

Tessy expressed her disbelief at the situation, admitting that even she hadn't expected such a drastic decision from the company's head office. But as she spoke, she saw Karthick's face contort with guilt and fear. It was evident that he carried heavy responsibilities – caring for his aging parents and now his new wife. He tearfully explained that without this job, he had no other means to support his family.

His words struck a chord with Tessy. She realized the gravity of the situation and the immense pressure Karthick was under. It pained her to see him so distraught, especially knowing that his wife's decision to marry him was contingent on his job security.

Feeling a mixture of empathy and helplessness, Tessy assured Karthick that she would do everything in her power to help him. However, she couldn't deny the harsh reality of the layoffs that had already begun.

With tear-filled eyes, Karthick thanked Tessy and left the cabin, leaving Tessy deep in thought. She pondered over why Karthick, typically reserved and composed, had broken down so completely in front of her. It was a stark contrast to the confident demeanour he usually displayed in the office.

As she watched Karthick leave, Tessy couldn't shake off the weight of the situation. She knew that the challenges ahead would be daunting, but she was determined to do whatever she could to support her team through these uncertain times.

As Tessy sat in the bus on her way home, her mind was filled with thoughts of Karthick and the sudden turn of events. She watched as Karthick, who usually exuded confidence, sat there in a very different manner, his demeanour now subdued and anxious. His tears still haunted her, and she couldn't shake off the image of him breaking down earlier in her office.

As the bus made its way through the bustling streets, Tessy found herself lost in her own memories. She reflected on her past life, the challenges she had faced, and the decisions she had made that led her to where she was today. Tessy's mind drifted back to the time when she first joined Coretronix Techno Solutions, filled with hope and ambition. She remembered the excitement of starting a new job and the challenges she had overcome to climb the ranks and become a respected team leader.

But now, as she faced the uncertainty of the layoffs, Tessy couldn't help but feel a sense of vulnerability. The suddenness of it all had caught her off guard, and she worried about the future not just for herself, but also for her team members like Karthick who depended on their jobs to support their families.

As the bus reached Tessy's apartment complex, she stepped off with a heavy heart. The evening sky was tinged with shades of orange and pink, casting a melancholic glow over the surroundings. Tessy took a deep breath and braced herself for the challenges that lay ahead.

Part 44

BONDING MOMENTS

As Tessy made adjustments in her daily routine to accommodate Amal's needs and ensure he felt supported, she found herself increasingly exhausted and unhappy. She wanted to ensure that Amal felt loved and secure, especially after the court proceedings where he stood by her side. However, her efforts seemed to backfire as Amal started to exhibit unruly behaviour at school, taking advantage of the extra attention he was receiving.

Tessy tried to maintain discipline and structure in their daily routine, but Amal's behaviour became increasingly challenging. He would act out in school, disrupting classes and getting into trouble with his teachers. Tessy felt overwhelmed by the constant need to manage Amal's behaviour while also juggling her responsibilities at work and home.

Despite her efforts, Tessy couldn't shake the feeling that she was artificially creating a situation where Amal received special treatment. She worried that this would only lead to further problems in the long run, both for Amal and for their family as a whole.

Sanjay, on the other hand, observed everything quietly. He could see the strain on his mother and the changes in his brother's behaviour. Sanjay tried to support his mother as much as he could, but he also struggled with the dynamics between Tessy and Amal. He doubts his mother's desire to protect and support Amal, but he also knew that it was important for Amal to learn to take responsibility for his actions.

As Tessy sat in Advocate Ramya's office, discussing the upcoming court hearing, she couldn't help but feel the weight of the situation on her shoulders. Amal sat beside her, asking for the mobile phone, and Tessy handed it to him, putting on a YouTube Kids video to keep him occupied. Sanjay joined his brother, and both boys became engrossed in watching their favourite series.

Tessy opened up to Ramya about her concerns regarding Amal's behaviour. "I know Amal has been acting out lately," Tessy began, "but I've been trying to support him until the next hearing."

Advocate Ramya listened attentively, her face showing understanding and empathy. "It's important to maintain some stability for Amal during this time," she agreed. "But we also need to work on setting boundaries and discipline. It's crucial for his well-being and for the case."

Tessy nodded, feeling a sense of relief knowing that Ramya understood her situation. She knew she needed to find a balance between supporting Amal and ensuring that he understood the consequences of his actions.

Sanjay, who had been listening to his mother's conversation with Advocate Ramya, began to realize the gravity of the situation.

He understood that his brother's behaviour was affecting their family's legal proceedings. Sanjay made a mental note to support his mother and help with Amal's discipline in the coming days.

Part 45

THE BURDEN OF PRETENSE

$\mathcal{A}$s the clock struck 8 PM, the living room was bathed in the soft glow of the television screen. Tessy sat on the couch, her posture tense, eyes fixed on the unfolding news broadcast. The newsreader's voice was sombre, conveying the gravity of the situation. "Breaking news: The coronavirus outbreak continues to spread rapidly across China. In response, the Chinese government has imposed lockdowns in several major cities, including Wuhan, Beijing, and Shanghai. Residents are being urged to stay indoors as authorities work tirelessly to contain the virus."

Meanwhile Sanjay sat at his study table, diligently working on his homework, while Amal was engrossed in creating paper crafts with colourful stickers. Tessy sees the children's study area and asked Sanjay what he was doing. Sanjay replied that he was studying, while Tessy noticed Amal's paper craft and the new pair of scissors he was using.

Tessy asked Amal where he got the new scissors from. Amal hesitated for a moment before replying that it was from his friend's mom. Tessy questioned further, asking how his friend's mom gave it to him. Amal then admitted that he didn't receive it from his friend's mom; instead, he took it without permission.

Tessy's heart sank as she realized her son had stolen the scissors. Shocked and disappointed, she scolded Amal sternly and began to punish him. The weight of the past month's sorrows and struggles came pouring out in her anger, and she ended up spanking Amal harder than she intended.

Amal started to cry, his body trembling with fear and guilt. Through his tears, he managed to choke out a heartfelt apology, but Tessy was too upset to accept it. She emphasized the seriousness of stealing, explaining to Amal that taking things without permission was wrong and sinful.

As Tessy struggled with her emotions, torn between her desire to discipline her son and her own inner turmoil, she couldn't help but cry out loud. Tears streamed down her face as she grappled with the weight of the past month's challenges. Despite her exhaustion, she made a silent vow to herself: "Whatever challenges come, I will accept."

Tessy sat alone in her living room, the weight of the situation pressing heavily on her shoulders. The events of the past month had taken their toll, and she felt like she was on the verge of breaking down. But amidst the chaos of her emotions, Tessy found a glimmer of hope. She believed that no matter how difficult things seemed now, she would find the strength to overcome them.

As she wiped away her tears, Tessy resolved to face the next day with renewed determination. She knew that whatever lay ahead, she would tackle it head-on. With a deep breath, she pushed aside her worries and focused on finding solutions to the challenges that lay before her. Tomorrow was a new day, and Tessy was determined to face it with courage and resilience.

Tessy couldn't shake the feeling that she was just acting her way through life. For the past month, she had been going through the motions, trying to keep up appearances for the sake of her children and herself. But deep down, she knew that she wasn't being true to herself.

Part 46

THE UNEXPECTED OUTCOME

FINAL VERDICT DAY 20TH DECEMBER 2019

Tessy stood before the judge, her heart heavy with tension and anxiety as she faced the prospect of divorce. Aravind stood opposite to her, his demeanour reflecting the sombre atmosphere of the courtroom. Their respective advocates, Ramya and Gulam, were ready to present their cases.

The judge, with a solemn expression on his face, addressed Tessy directly, asking if she was prepared for mutual divorce. Tessy, her voice trembling slightly, managed to affirm her readiness. The judge then turned to Ramya, Tessy's advocate, and inquired about her client's willingness to give one child to her husband.

Ramya responded with a request to allow the children to express their preferences. She explained that Tessy's decision was influenced by the children's desires, as they were the ones directly affected by the situation. The judge, recognizing the validity of Ramya's argument, accepted her request.

Aravind's advocate, Gulam, attempted to object, but the judge did not grant his objection. Instead, the judge agreed to ask the children themselves whom they wished to live with.

Tessy felt a mix of relief and apprehension as the judge's decision unfolded. She knew that allowing the children to choose would be the fairest option, but she also feared the outcome. Deep down, she hoped her children would choose to stay with her, but she was prepared to accept whatever decision they made.

Sanjay stood before the judge, his young face reflecting a mixture of confusion, sadness, and determination. The judge, with a compassionate yet firm tone, explained to him the reason for the court proceedings.

The respected judge addressed Sanjay, acknowledging his status as the elder one, stating that he trusted Sanjay to understand the gravity of the situation and make a thoughtful decision, as the judge's decision would be based on Sanjay's response.

"Sanjay, your parents want to separate, and the court is going to grant them a divorce. Your daddy needs one son with him," the respected judge said, looking directly at Sanjay.

Sanjay listened intently, his mind swirling with thoughts and emotions. When the judge asked him the crucial question of whom he wanted to live with, Sanjay remained silent, processing the weight of the decision before him.

The judge repeated the question, urging Sanjay to choose between his parents. Sanjay's gaze shifted between his father, standing with a sombre expression, and his mother, whose eyes were filled with anticipation and anxiety.

After a few moments of contemplation, Sanjay's face lifted, and he boldly declared, "I want to live with both."

The courtroom fell into a stunned silence. Even Aravind, Sanjay's father, appeared taken aback by his son's response. The judge, surprised by Sanjay's answer, asked again, offering him another chance to choose.

But Sanjay's determination grew stronger as he spoke again, his voice tinged with frustration and anger. "I want to live with my both father and mother!" he exclaimed. "Who are you to separate my mom and daddy? I want to live with both!"

Tessy, overwhelmed with emotion, watched her son bravely stand up for what he believed was right. His words pierced through the tension in the courtroom, echoing the pain of a child caught in the midst of his parent's separation.

Sanjay's bold and angry reply reverberated in the courtroom, leaving everyone momentarily stunned. However, the judge remained composed, unfazed by Sanjay's outburst. He calmly took a sip of water and passed the bottle to his assistants.

"Sanjay," the judge began, his voice steady, "I am here to make judgments. That's my job, Respected Judge smiled because of Sanjay's innocence.

Sanjay's anger seemed to dissipate as he listened to the judge's words. His gaze softened, and he realized the gravity of the situation.

The courtroom fell into a tense silence as the judge called for a brief recess, indicating that the session would resume in the afternoon. As everyone filed out of the courtroom, Sanjay lingered for a moment, his mind still swirling with emotions.

As advocate Gulam discussed the unexpected turn of events with Aravind, Aravind couldn't help but smile at the thought of his elder son standing up for him. "It's a great twist indeed," Gulam remarked, trying to reassure Aravind. "Most probably, your younger son will mention your name.

Aravind nodded, feeling a glimmer of hope amidst the uncertainty. "If it leads to divorce, please try to stop it," Aravind requested, his voice tinged with concern.

Meanwhile, Tessy paced nervously outside the courtroom, her mind consumed with worry about Sanjay's upcoming testimony. "Why did he say both?" she thought to herself anxiously. "He never mentioned wanting to live with both of us before."

Part 47

ONE LAST REQUEST

*I*n Advocate Ramya's office, Tessy sat with her children, anxiously waiting for Ramya to discuss the afternoon session. Sanjay stood by his mother, a mix of fear and determination evident in his demeanour, while Amal played nearby, oblivious to the tension in the room.

After some time, Tessy, growing impatient, asked Sanjay why he had said "both" earlier, her voice tinged with mild anger. Sanjay remained silent, his expression calm but resolute. Tessy's frustration grew, and she asked again, this time with more intensity, demanding a response.

When Sanjay still didn't reply, Tessy raised her voice, shouting his name. Sanjay finally spoke, his voice steady but firm, "I want to be with both of you. I need you both."

Tessy's heart clenched at her son's words, but she quickly dismissed his request, saying it was not possible. She had endured countless struggles and tears alone, and she couldn't bear the thought of facing them again.

Just then, Advocate Ramya entered the room, sensing the tension. With her calming presence, she diffused the situation, gently reassuring Tessy and soothing Sanjay's fears. Sanjay remained silent, his eyes downcast, as Ramya guided them through the upcoming session.

As the discussion continued, Tessy couldn't shake off the weight of her son's words.

Ramya observed Tessy's distress and asked her why her son was behaving in a certain way. Tessy remained silent, unable to find the words to explain.

Understanding the urgency of the situation, Ramya assured Tessy that they needed to focus on the afternoon session as it was crucial for their case. She instructed Tessy to make necessary arrangements and prepare for what lay ahead.

Ramya emphasized the importance of the session, reminding Tessy that they were on the verge of obtaining the divorce order. She assured Tessy that despite the challenges they faced, they would prevail.

"Today, we will secure the divorce order," Ramya declared confidently. "We can't afford to waste any time. This afternoon session is our opportunity to strengthen our case."

Though Tessy felt uncertain and overwhelmed, she nodded in agreement, trusting Ramya's guidance. Ramya continued, explaining that during the session, they needed to ensure that Amal's responses would support their case.

"We need to train Amal to respond in a way that reflects positively on you," Ramya explained. "His answers will influence the judge's decision, so we must prepare him accordingly."

Tessy listened attentively, her confusion slowly giving way to determination. Despite her doubts, she found solace in Ramya's unwavering support and determination.

With a renewed sense of purpose, Tessy began to make the necessary arrangements for the afternoon session, knowing that it was their best chance to secure a favourable outcome. As they prepared to face the challenges ahead, Tessy found strength in Ramya's words and the knowledge that they were not alone in their fight.

Amal sat quietly, engrossed in the mobile phone, while Sanjay stood nearby, his expression filled with fear. Advocate Ramya, noticing the tense atmosphere, decided to lighten the mood by offering chocolates to the boys. Amal eagerly grabbed a handful of chocolates and offered one to Sanjay, who hesitated to accept it.

Seeing Sanjay's reluctance, Amal forcefully took a chocolate from Ramya's hand and handed it to his brother. Ramya smiled at their interaction and decided to take Amal aside for a moment.

Outside the office, Ramya spoke to Amal in a gentle yet firm tone. She explained to him the importance of his decision during the upcoming court session. "Listen carefully, Amal," she said. "Today, the judge will ask you whom you want to go with. If you choose to go with your mom, she will always love and care for you, and she will never hurt you."

Amal listened eagerly, his eyes shining with excitement as he clutched his handful of chocolates. Ramya reiterated, "When the judge asks you, remember to say that you want to go with your mom."

With a bright smile, Amal nodded in understanding. He felt reassured by Ramya's words and eagerly anticipated the chance to express his choice.

As they returned to the office, Amal's excitement was palpable. When the judge asked him the crucial question, Amal didn't hesitate for a moment. With confidence, he replied, "I want to go with my mom."

Advocate Ramya smiled proudly as she watched Amal make his decision. She knew that his choice would have a significant impact on their case, and she was grateful for his courage and trust in her guidance.

After Advocate Ramya returned to her consulting room, Amal went back to the table where he was watching his mobile with his brother, Sanjay. Advocate Ramya smiled at Tessy reassuringly, telling her not to worry and that the divorce procedure would be finished that day.

Meanwhile, outside the room, Amal was deeply engrossed in his mobile, his expression serious. Sanjay, curious about what Advocate Ramya had said, asked Amal repeatedly, but Amal remained silent. Sensing Amal's reluctance to speak, Sanjay softened his voice and gently asked again. Amal finally opened up and explained everything that Advocate Ramya had told him.

As Amal shared the details, Sanjay's fear began to rise. He realized that a deep discussion was going on inside the room where his mom and Advocate Ramya were. Sanjay knew that the outcome of this discussion would have a significant impact on their family's future.

Sanjay's voice trembled as he approached Amal, his eyes glistening with tears. "Amal, please, just one minute," he pleaded softly, but Amal continued to focus on his mobile. With persistence, Sanjay urged Amal again, his voice cracking with emotion. Finally, Amal looked up, sensing the urgency in his brother's tone. "Tell me, I'm listening," he said, his curiosity piqued.

Sanjay took a deep breath, trying to steady his trembling voice. "Amal, please, whatever I say, don't shout. Just listen," he implored. "Mom and Dad, they're both important to us. We need them both."

Sanjay's voice grew more emotional as he continued, tears streaming down his cheeks. "Our parents mean everything to us, Amal. Please, just this once, listen to me. If the judge asks you who you want to go with, say you need both of them. Please, Amal, for me."

Amal hesitated, considering Sanjay's words carefully. Finally, he shook his head. "No, I won't say that," he replied stubbornly.

Sanjay's eyes widened in dismay, but he remained composed. "Fine, Amal," he said calmly, wiping his tears away. "I won't say anything to mom. You can do whatever you want in school, and in life. I won't ever complain. But please, understand, Amal.

From now on, I'll give you all my toys, chocolates—anything I get. Just please, tell the judge you need both parents."

Sanjay's voice broke as he made his final plea, tears flowing freely. Meanwhile, the door to the discussion room opened, and Tessy emerged. Sanjay quickly wiped his tears, trying to compose himself, while Amal watched silently. Tessy gathered her sons, and they left for the courtroom together, unaware of the difficult decision looming ahead.

Part 48

GOD'S VERDICT

As the afternoon session approached, both Aravind and Tessy entered the courtroom, each lost in their own thoughts and anxieties. The atmosphere inside the courtroom was tense as they took their seats, waiting for the proceedings to resume.

In the courtroom, the tension was palpable as the judge addressed Sanjay, asking if he was still standing by his decision. Sanjay remained silent, his head bowed slightly as he softly replied, "Yes."

The judge, after a moment of deep thought, called out to Amal, who was sitting quietly in a corner with his mother. As a 6-year-old child, Amal walked timidly into the courtroom, staying close to his mother, his eyes filled with fear.

The judge then asked Amal to come forward. But Amal, feeling overwhelmed, shook his head and whispered, "I stand with my mom." The judge gently explained to Amal that his parents wanted to separate and asked for his decision on whom he wanted to live with.

Amal, unsure and confused, stood silently, his face reflecting his inner turmoil. Sensing Amal's hesitation, the judge asked again, urging him to choose between his father and mother.

Amal looked around the courtroom, his eyes darting between his mother, his father, and his brother Sanjay. He thought about his mother's care and love, his brother's request, and his father's presence.

The judge repeated the question, "Whom do you want to live with, father or mother? Tell any name, and you can go with them now."

Amal struggled to find the words, torn between his love for both his parents. Finally, he replied softly, "I want to live with both." Amal echoed what his brother Sanjay had said earlier. His words echoed through the courtroom, surprising everyone present.

Sanjay, overwhelmed with emotion, ran to his brother Amal and hugged him tightly, tears streaming down his cheeks. He kissed Amal's forehead, expressing his love and gratitude for his little brother.

The judge smiled warmly at Amal's response, ignoring Gulam's objections. He looked at Advocate Ramya and nodded, acknowledging the maturity of the children.

Aravind watched in astonishment, his face filled with excitement and pride at his sons' display of love and maturity. Tessy, overwhelmed by the moment, didn't know how to react. She locked eyes with Aravind, and in that moment, they shared a silent understanding and love.

Tessy's heart swelled with pride and love for her children, realizing their maturity and unconditional love for both parents. She smiled lightly at Aravind, her eyes brimming with tears of joy and gratitude.

The respected judge observed everything and announced that the court would adjourn for the day, scheduling the next hearing in two months. With that, the afternoon court session came to an end.

"Time will change everything"

GSG

Thank you

TO MY READERS,

Thank you for joining me in exploring the obstacles of human life. I hope the characters Sanjay and Amal resonated with you and touched your inner emotions, just as they did for me.

If you enjoyed this book, I would be truly grateful if you could spare a minute to leave a short review on the page or site where you purchased the book. Your help in spreading the word is greatly appreciated!

Thank you! You're amazing too!

With profound gratitude,

GSG

Acknowledgements

First and foremost, I want to express my gratitude to my wife, who has been incredibly supportive throughout the process of writing my story. As someone who struggles with English communication and writing, especially in story format, her understanding of how I narrate stories in my mother tongue has been invaluable. With her guidance and the aid of today's technology, she helped me craft this book.

I also want to extend my thanks to my friend, who served as the inspiration behind this story.

Great thanks to my parents and my children for their unwavering love and encouragement throughout this journey.

Author Bio

G.S. Gunanidhi, aged 35, was working as an assistant professor in the computer science and engineering department, but for the past three years, he has been struggling with physical illness. This constant battle left him tired all the time, and he reached a point where he felt unable to continue his job. Despite his challenges, storytelling has always been a passion since his young age. He found solace in creating his own stories, which often helped him navigate difficult situations, including times when he had to lie to his parents.

Now, facing another turning point in his life, he realizes that storytelling could once again be his lifeline.

You can connect with him at **gsgnovelist.03@gmail.com**.

www.ingramcontent.com/pod-product-compliance
Lightning Source LLC
LaVergne TN
LVHW041707070526
838199LV00045B/1243